GEORGE WASHINGTON CARVER

FOR KIDS

His Life and Discoveries, with 21 Activities

PEGGY THOMAS

CHICAGO
REVIEW
PRESS

Copyright © 2019 by Peggy Thomas
All rights reserved
Published by Chicago Review Press Incorporated
814 North Franklin Street
Chicago, Illinois 60610
ISBN 978-0-915864-00-3

Library of Congress Cataloging-in-Publication Data

Names: Thomas, Peggy, 1960– author.
Title: George Washington Carver for kids : his life and discoveries with 21
    activities / Peggy Thomas.
Description: Chicago, Illinois : Chicago Review Press Incorporated, [2019] |
    Audience: Age 9. | Audience: Grades 4 to 6. | Includes bibliographical
    references and index.
Identifiers: LCCN 2018035154 (print) | LCCN 2018035951 (ebook) | ISBN
    9780915864041 (Pdf) | ISBN 9780915864058 (Epub) | ISBN 9780915864102
    (Kindle) | ISBN 9780915864003 (trade paper)
Subjects: LCSH: Carver, George Washington, 1864?–1943—Juvenile
    literature. | Tuskegee Institute—History—Juvenile literature. |
    African American agriculturists—Biography—Juvenile literature. |
    Agriculturists—United States—Biography—Juvenile literature. | African
    American scientists—Biography—Juvenile literature. | Scientists—
    Biography—Juvenile literature.
Classification: LCC S417.C3 (ebook) | LCC S417.C3 T485 2019 (print) | DDC
    630.92 [B] —dc23
LC record available at https://lccn.loc.gov/2018035154

Cover design: Jonathan Hahn
Cover images: (front, clockwise from top right) Carver in his lab, *Tuskegee
    University Archives, Tuskegee University*; Tuskegee University seal, *photo by
    author*; preserved fruits and vegetables, *photo by author*; Carver teaching
    a botany class, *Tuskegee University Archives, Tuskegee University*; peanuts,
    Krzysztof Puszczyński/Pexels; (back, clockwise from top right) Carver tends
    to plants, *Tuskegee University Archives, Tuskegee University*; Carver the artist,
    courtesy of the George Washington Carver National Monument; gourd activity,
    illustration by Lindsey Cleworth Schauer
Interior design: Sarah Olson
Interior illustrations: Lindsey Cleworth Schauer

Printed in the United States of America
5 4 3 2 1

CONTENTS

TIME LINE

1864–65 George Washington Carver born in Diamond Grove, Missouri

1876 Attends school in Neosho, Missouri

1879 Travels to Fort Scott, Kansas

1880 Moves to Minneapolis, Kansas

1885 Rejected from Highland College (Kansas)

1886 Homesteads in Beeler, Kansas

1888 Moves to Winterset, Iowa

1890 Enrolls at Simpson College, Indianola, Iowa

1891 Student at Iowa Agricultural College, Ames, Iowa

1893 Painting wins honorable mention at the World's Columbian Exposition in Chicago

1894 Graduates from Iowa and becomes first black faculty member

1896 Becomes director of agricultural department at Tuskegee Institute, Alabama

1906 Creates the Jesup Wagon

1916 Member of the British Royal Society of Arts

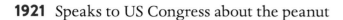

1921 Speaks to US Congress about the peanut

1933 Works with polio patients

1935 Collaborates with USDA on mycology research

Austin Curtis arrives in Tuskegee

1937 Speaks at chemurgy conference in Dearborn, Michigan

1941 Opens the George Washington Carver Museum

1943 Dies January 5 in Tuskegee, Alabama

George Washington Carver.
Tuskegee University Archives, Tuskegee University

ALL THAT IS KNOWN

No individual has any right to come into the world and go out of it without leaving behind him distinct and legitimate reasons for having passed through it. —George Washington Carver

---

Today, most Americans recycle paper, plastic, and metal cans. We use biodegradable shopping bags and may even compost our kitchen scraps. Our cars are built with soybean plastic parts, and fueled by corn-based ethanol. George Washington Carver would be pleased. He spent most of his life promoting conservation and developing new products from agriculture.

"Thenceforward, and forever free." —Emancipation Proclamation. *Courtesy of the Library of Congress, LC-DIG-pga-02040*

These ideas seem commonplace today, but they were unusual 100 years ago. There were plenty of natural resources, and farmers just focused on growing food and fiber crops without worrying about whether they were using those resources efficiently. But Carver saw a lot was going to waste, and he met too many poor farmers who could barely feed themselves as a result. He had to do something. Carver's work in conservation and agriculture was all part of a bigger vision. He saw a world where people lived in harmony with nature and with each other. This vision began long before he became famous for developing dozens of peanut products. It was rooted in a lifetime of struggle and uncertainty. George struggled against poverty and racism, and was uncertain about who he was, what he could be, and where he came from.

Born in Diamond Grove, near present-day Diamond, Missouri, Carver never knew his father, his mother, or even the day he was born. "As nearly as I can trace my history," he said, "I was about two weeks old when the war closed."

Carver was referring to the Civil War, the most divisive and violent event in US history. Although a tiny baby at the time, the war had a profound impact on his life, and he would carry the emotional scars always. In a sense, the war was all about Carver and millions of people like him—enslaved African Americans.

When Abraham Lincoln won the 1860 election pledging to end slavery in the western territories, seven Southern states broke away—seceded— from the North and formed the Confederate States

Carver's Birthday—Deciphering the Record

Depending on what book you read, George Washington Carver's birthday could be anywhere between 1860 and 1865. When Carver lived in Kansas, he stated that he was born in 1865, but later in life he grew elusive and claimed he was born near the end of the war, or when "freedom was declared." But that could mean many things. President Lincoln issued the Emancipation Proclamation freeing slaves in Confederate states on September 22, 1862, and it was put into effect January 1, 1863. The Civil War, however, ended in April 1865. To complicate matters, the border state of Missouri officially abolished slavery three months earlier, in January.

For decades, historians based Carver's birth on a US census taken in 1870. It listed George as 10 years old and born in 1860. Who was right? It seems unlikely that his surrogate father, who probably provided the information, could confuse a five-year-old with a ten-year-old, but it would be even stranger if Carver were wrong. Did the census taker make a mistake?

The debate over Carver's birth was not just about accuracy in history. It was about slavery. Was he born a slave or free? If he had been an ordinary guy, no one would have cared, but George became famous and his transformation from slave to scientist was an important, inspirational story to tell. It highlighted the potential inside every African American. It forecast all the marvelous achievements to come and made people wonder about the great things that could have happened if millions of men, women, and children had not been brutally demeaned and enslaved. But it must have been frustrating to Carver as he grew more famous. In response to one request for information, he wrote, "This is all that is known about my early life. I presume it is difficult for you to appreciate the fact that a slave child was nothing but chattel and no record was kept of their birth."

Today, Carver's story stands on its own merits. But still, people want to know a date. In 1952, the US Congress designated July 12, 1860, as George's birthday, but the National Park Service, which oversees the George Washington Carver National Monument in Diamond, Missouri, cites 1864 in its brochure. Unless more evidence is unearthed, his birthday will forever remain a mystery.

One thing we do know about the man without a birthday: dates mattered to George. Before he read any letter, document, or memo, he wrote the day's date along the top of the page.

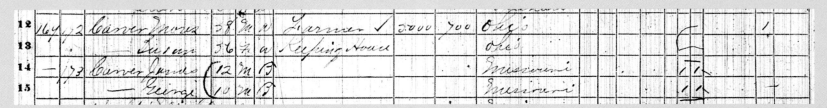

1870 US census listing George as 10 years old. *Courtesy of the State Historical Society of Missouri*

of America. Four more proslavery states would eventually join them after the Battle of Fort Sumter on April 12, 1861. For four bloody years the Union and Confederate Armies clashed in combat until April 1865, when the South surrendered, and all slaves, including baby George, were set free.

The Carver Homestead

The farm where George was born was owned by Moses Carver, one of the first settlers adventurous enough to stake a claim deep in the southwest corner of the new state of Missouri. The Preemption Act of 1841 promised Moses and other men that if they lived on and improved 160 acres of public land for at least six months, they could buy the property for the rock-bottom price of $1.25 an acre. Moses

Carver chose his site carefully: a plot with fertile prairie for grazing, forest for timber, and plenty of water from a creek and two springs. Eventually, he came to own 240 acres of prime farmland.

Staking a claim was backbreaking work, but Moses and his wife, Susan, were determined. First they cleared a patch of land near the creek, burning brush and digging roots. They felled timber and carefully notched and stacked the rough-hewn logs to make a cabin. Like most homesteaders, the Carvers used clay, called chinking, to pack the gaps between the logs and constructed a clapboard roof. When they were done, the cabin measured a mere 12 feet by 12 feet, but it had all they needed: a fireplace for cooking, a window for light, and an easy-to-sweep hard-packed dirt floor. After Moses took in his orphaned niece and two nephews, that

(below) **Moses Carver.** *Tuskegee University Archives, Tuskegee University*

(right) **Site of the Carvers' log cabin, where George was born.** *Photo by author*

4

small cabin housed a family of five for a number of years. With the extra help, Moses cleared more land and planted acres of Indian corn, wheat, oats, hay, flax, and potatoes.

Each year, the Carvers' farm grew. At the center of all the activity stood a large barn that sheltered several horses. According to neighbors, Moses Carver had a gift for working with animals and training racehorses, which was an unusual profession in the frontier at that time. Beyond the barn, stock pens made of split-rail fencing corralled pigs, sheep, and cattle. The Carvers milked cows and made cider from apples picked in their orchard. Susan tended the kitchen garden, raised chickens, washed laundry, mended clothes, and cooked the meals.

On rare occasions the family would trek to the general store several miles away, and then only to mail a letter or purchase luxury items like sugar or coffee. Everything else they grew, made themselves, or took from the abundant land they lived on. Moses went out at dawn often to hunt deer and wild turkey, while Susan collected wild berries and edible plants. Nothing went to waste. When Moses mucked out the horse stalls, the manure was composted and used to fertilize the fields. Susan saved dried-out gourds from the garden to serve as bowls, cups, and ladles. Even their bees did double duty pollinating the fields and providing honey. At the end of a long hard day the Carvers retired to a house no bigger than a modern bedroom. By 1855, however, their niece and nephews were grown and gone. Moses and Susan needed more help.

Moses Carver (1812–1910)

Moses Carver was born on August 29, 1812, in Dayton, Ohio. His parents were of German descent, and he inherited their capacity for hard work. In 1834 Carver married Susan Blue in Springfield, Illinois. Shortly after, the young couple moved west to Missouri, along with Moses's two brothers. Friends remember Moses Carver as being frugal with money but generous with his labor. He loved music and carried a pet rooster on his shoulder.

Headstone of Moses Carver.
Photo by author

Headstone of Susan Carver.
Photo by author

Turn a Gourd into a Bowl

Moses and Susan Carver created some of their kitchen utensils from gourds, which are similar to squash and pumpkins. After harvest, the gourds are left to dry instead of being eaten. Depending on the size of the gourd, it can be turned into a spoon, ladle, plate, or bowl.

ADULT SUPERVISION REQUIRED

YOU'LL NEED

- Dried gourd (they come in all shapes and sizes—find one that will stand up, like a bottle gourd)
- Scrubby sponge
- Pencil
- Cup or jar
- Serrated bread knife or pumpkin-carving tool
- Adult helper
- Spoon
- Sandpaper (fine to medium grit)
- Paint or polyurethane

1. Clean the gourd: scrub the gourd with a dry, rough sponge to remove dirt and debris. Brown spots will not come off, they will become part of the decoration.

2. Mark a cutting line. To make an even line, secure a pencil on a cup or jar that is just the right height for the top of your bowl. With the pencil tip touching the gourd, turn the gourd slowly and you will get a level, even line.

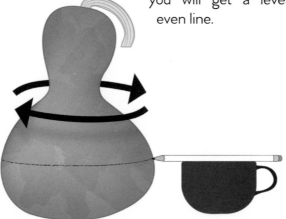

3. Cut the gourd with an adult's help. Place a knife along the cutting line and slowly cut into the gourd using a sawing motion. Work your way around the gourd. **Be careful not to press too hard**—the gourd is brittle and may crack.

4. Clean inside. Take off the top of your gourd and pull out the seeds and other dried material. Scrape the inside surface with a spoon until smooth.

5. Sand the cut edge. Place the gourd open side down on a sheet of sandpaper. Move the gourd across the sandpaper in gentle circular motions until the rim of your bowl is smooth.

6. Finish by decorating your bowl with paint, or leave it natural and spray with a coat of clear polyurethane.

The Missouri Compromise

The state of Missouri came into American hands when Thomas Jefferson purchased the Louisiana Territory from France in 1803. Wagon trains of settlers moved west, and in 1812 a portion of the Louisiana Purchase was sectioned off and named the Missouri Territory. William Clark, of the Lewis and Clark Expedition, became the first governor.

Six years later, Missouri applied to the federal government for statehood. The hot-button issue around statehood was whether a state allowed or opposed slavery. At the time, there were 11 slave states and 11 free states in the Union. In order to maintain this delicate stability, the government sought a compromise: Maine was admitted as a free state, and on August 10, 1821, Missouri became a slave state.

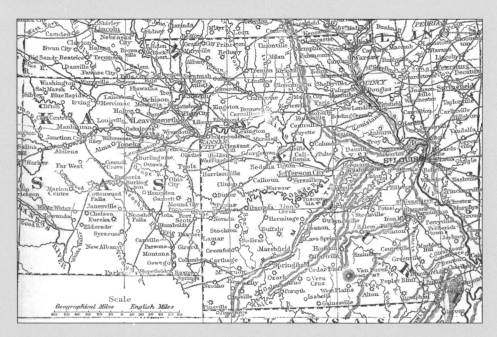

Map of Missouri. *Courtesy of Documenting the American South, UNC–Chapel Hill Library*

Mary, "A Slave for Life"

On Tuesday, October 9, 1855, Moses Carver met with William P. McGinnis, a prosperous neighbor who owned at least seven slaves: six males and one female. Moses purchased a "negro girl named Mary age about thirteen years." John Dade Jr. served as witness for the deal. On the bill of sale, McGinnis assured Carver that Mary was "sound in body and mind and a slave for life." Moses paid $700 for the girl who would become George's mother.

If McGinnis hadn't been willing to sell, Moses Carver might have had to travel to a distant city like St. Louis, where there were several slave markets. He would have had to view the "property" crammed into one of two slave pens before they went up for auction. Would he have done what other prospective buyers often did and inspect the men and women's feet, limbs, hair, and teeth? He certainly would have heard the thwack of the auctioneer's gavel, and the cries and pleading as children were torn away from their parents, and husbands were separated from their wives.

The purchase of Mary may have been more neighborly, but it was no less inhumane. We can only imagine the fear in Mary's heart as she left the only family she had known and traveled against her will to her new home on the Carver farm.

The fact that Moses Carver bought her at all is often portrayed as out of character. Many biographies of George Washington Carver claim that Moses Carver was a slaveholding abolitionist who supported the Union. But there is no evidence of this except that he was born in the free state of

Ohio and had lived in the same town as Abraham Lincoln in Illinois. If he was against slavery, why would he ignore his upbringing to buy Mary? Was there some other reason for the transaction? We may never know. We do know, however, that slaveholding was a sign of wealth in Newton County, Missouri, and Moses Carver became one of only five farmers in the region to own a slave.

Moses Carver acquired Mary during one of the busiest times of the year, harvest season. As the only slave on the property Mary probably worked alongside Susan and Moses from dawn to dusk cutting cornstalks, bundling flax, and stacking wheat into pyramids called shocks. Grain had to be threshed, and Mary would have spent long hours beating it with a hickory stick. Like other female slaves at the time, she helped with domestic chores, too, cooking, washing, and making clothes. Years later, her son George was given the spinning wheel that his mother used to spin wool and flax into thread.

Mary lived in the Carvers' old cabin. They had since upgraded to a new log home, only slightly bigger than the original. Soon she would fill it with her own family. Accounts suggest that Mary had several children, but slaveholders rarely kept accurate slave records, and Moses Carver was no exception. An enslaved child might be added to the farm inventory like a new horse or wagon, but if a child died young, which often happened, she might not be counted at all. Even as an adult, George Washington Carver was confused as to how many siblings he may have had. Once he said he had three sisters who died, and another time

The bill of sale for George's mother, Mary. *Tuskegee University Archives, Tuskegee University*

A slave auction in the South. *Courtesy of the Library of Congress, LC-USZ62-2582*

he said he had two. Only one of Mary's births was recorded: on October 10, 1859, Mary had a healthy baby boy named James.

While doing chores Mary looked after her son James, carrying him into the fields or plopping him down near the washbasin. She may have wished he'd always stay little, because when he was old enough he'd be given his own chores to do. When Jim was four or five, Mary had another son. She named him George.

George's Father

George Washington Carver believed that his father had been another slave who lived on a neighboring farm belonging to James Grant. "I am told that my father was killed while hauling wood with an ox team," he said. "In some way he fell from the load, under the wagon, both wheels passing over him."

Although slaves were allowed to marry, their marriages were not recognized legally, and married couples were often split up by slaveholders. Informal unions between slaves from different farms were called "abroad" marriages. Mary may have had this sort of arrangement with George's father.

Antislavery Jayhawker raiders. *Courtesy of the Library of Congress, LC-USZ62-100061*

Kidnapped

One night shortly after George was born, Moses Carver heard raiders on horseback crashing through the fields. He knew what they were after and ran to Mary's cabin. Even though the war was officially over, the citizens of Missouri were still fiercely divided. Those from the South had supported the Confederacy, while settlers from the East had sided with the Union. As a result, roving bands of raiders from both sides fought for control of the area. Unionist "Jayhawkers" swooped in from Kansas, and Bushwhackers terrorized from the South. They looted farms, stole or killed livestock, and kidnapped women and children.

That night, Moses Carver reached the cabin in time to grab Jim and hide behind a brush pile. He was too late to save Mary. She had already been wrenched off her feet by a raider and carried away, still desperately clutching tiny George to her chest.

This hadn't been the first time the Carver farm had been attacked. On at least three other occasions, Bushwhackers or Jayhawkers had stormed onto the property. In 1863 bandits demanded all of Moses Carver's money, which he kept buried around the yard. Stubbornly, he refused. The men strung him up and tortured him by pressing hot coals to the soles of his feet. When the bandits came up empty-handed after searching the property, they released Carver and left.

This time they had taken Mary and George. It is unclear what Moses Carver was thinking when he made his next move. Was he just bent on getting his hired hand back, or did he sincerely care for the welfare of Mary and her baby? Whatever his reason, the next morning Carver hired a Union scout named John Bentley to find the mother and son. He promised Bentley a fine horse for his efforts and gave him $300 to use as ransom. Bentley followed the Bushwhackers' trail down to Arkansas and found the child. Bentley wrapped the baby in his coat, tied him to the saddle, and hurried back to Diamond Grove. Mary was never seen again. Some people claimed she was sold back into bondage. Others said she escaped to the North, but would a mother voluntarily leave her child after a brutal kidnapping?

The baby that Bentley handed over to Susan Carver when he returned to Diamond Grove shook with violent bouts of whooping cough, a deadly disease back then, before the discovery of antibiotics. "I was so very frail and sick that they thought of course that I would die within a few days," George said. Moses moved the boys into the main cabin, and Susan nursed George back to health, spoon-feeding him herbal remedies and rubbing his tiny body with healing lotions. George recovered, but the whooping cough and other childhood ailments permanently damaged his vocal cords and left him with a high-pitched, raspy voice. All his life he was fragile and prone to illness. He lost his voice frequently and suffered from pernicious anemia, a condition where his body did not produce enough red blood cells.

George (left) and Jim Carver. *Tuskegee University Archives, Tuskegee University*

The Home Folks

Jim grew tall and strong and followed in Moses Carver's footsteps, learning to handle the oxen and work in the field. George thrived under Susan's care. He shadowed her throughout the day. Although the boys were no longer slaves, they still worked hard as children living on a frontier farm. George fetched water from the creek, his spindly arms straining with the weight. He fed the chickens and pumped a butter churn much taller

Washing day demonstration at George Washington Carver National Monument. *George Washington Carver National Monument*

From Ashes to Soap

Making soap was not something George would do for himself until he was much older, because it was a dangerous business. The Carvers would have collected ashes from the fireplace and dumped them into a leaching barrel or ash hopper, a large container with small holes in the bottom, along with leaves and rainwater. George remembered that "as a little boy . . . [he] carr[ied] gallons of water from . . . [the] spring for more than an hour to start the ash hopper running during the spring season to make the usual quantity of soap we needed for the year." This mixture was left to sit until lye (sodium hydroxide) dripped out of the holes into a bucket beneath the barrel. Lye is highly toxic and dissolves fat. Think about how a drop of dish soap breaks up gobs of grease on a plate. The lye was then mixed with lard or tallow—fat from a pig or cow—and left to sit and solidify. After many weeks it was cut into bars of soap.

than he was. Susan called on him to pick elderberries in the summer and apples in the fall. Everyone helped with sheep shearing, and George remembered they "scoured the wool, spun it, reeled it, and wove it into cloth right in our own home on a handmade loom." Harvest kept George particularly busy. He recalled sitting in the shade of the barn and shucking corn for hours.

Susan taught George how to fill a washbasin with water heated over the fire, add homemade lye soap, and wash clothes until his fingers pruned. His hands turned purple when he helped Susan dye freshly spun yarn or fabric with pokeberries he gathered from the woods. The pokeberry dye produced a warm, deep red, but they could also make brown or tan dye with tree bark, and yellow dye from onion skins or goldenrod flowers. George was also a quick study with recipes for stews and bread and learned to cook chicken for their Sunday dinner. His long nimble fingers mastered sewing, knitting, and crocheting as well. "I never saw anybody do anything with his hands that I couldn't do with mine," he said years later.

An example of George's lacework. *Photo by author*

When they weren't working, George and Jim played with the Carvers' grandnieces and nephews who lived nearby. One of the nephews, named Thomas Carver, became George's "dearest boyhood playmate." During those early years, George rarely saw other African Americans. Although he was an orphan, he didn't seem to let the atrocities of the past and the horrors his mother and father suffered cloud his youth. He remembered the Carvers fondly, writing in a letter to Thomas's daughter, "Indeed you really are my home folks."

The Carvers never had children of their own, so becoming surrogate parents again may have filled an empty part in their hearts as well. In the evenings the Carver family gathered by the fireplace. Moses—or Uncle Mose, as George sometimes called him—played the violin or told stories about his time in Illinois and living near Abraham Lincoln. In the dim candlelight, Susan taught George to read from the only book she owned, *Webster's Elementary Spelling Book*. "I almost knew the book by heart," George said. But that thin blue book did not have the answers to all the questions that ran through his head.

One night when the Carvers were asleep, the curious boys snuck out of the house to explore in the dark. Susan soon found them and threatened Jim and George with a spanking. It was Moses who calmed her down and saved them the punishment. The only time George remembered being harshly treated was when he and Jim rode a sheep. They had already been warned once, so Moses gave them a thrashing to make sure they would not do it again. For the most part, Susan did her best to teach George good manners, and throughout his life he was remembered for his kind and gentle ways.

The Plant Doctor

Each morning before his chores began, George wandered off into the woods to think and wonder. It would become a lifelong habit. "I literally lived in the woods," he said. "I wanted to know every strange stone, flower, insect, bird, or beast." The creek that ran behind the house held minnows, crayfish, and frogs to catch, while nuthatches, wrens, and robins flitted high in the redbud and oak trees. As the seasons changed, George noticed how bugs and other creatures changed as well. In summer the buzz of cicadas served as the soundtrack to his busy thoughts, but in winter his ideas quietly swished and swirled with the dry leaves overhead.

George didn't just think on his morning walks, he observed, explored, and picked up anything that sparked his curiosity. One fall day he brought home a milkweed pod, and it exploded inside the cabin. Hundreds of fuzzy seeds floated in the air and clung to the freshly washed clothes. To prevent any more mishaps, Susan demanded that George empty his pockets at the door. After that, George kept most of his treasures outside. He collected rocks, and wondered how some came to be striped and others speckled with sparkly crystals. He squirreled away his rock collection beside the chimney, but when the pile grew too large Susan made him throw some away. "I obeyed," he wrote

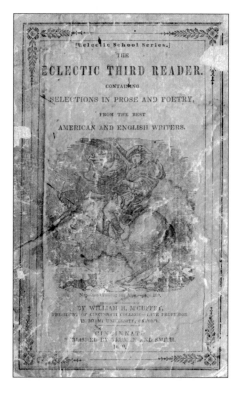

Generations of children learned how to read and write using Noah Webster's spelling and grammar books. *Department of Special Collections, Stanford University Libraries*

MAKE A CROSS-STITCH SAMPLER

When George was small, Susan Carver would have shown him how to sew a basic cross-stitch, and he would have practiced by sewing a sampler on whatever material they had lying around, such as old burlap sacks that had a loose weave, which allowed him to easily count his stitches.

YOU'LL NEED

- Burlap (⅓ yard)
- Scissors
- Fine-point marker
- Embroidery thread in a variety of colors
- Needle with large eye

1. Cut a 10-by-12-inch rectangle of burlap.

2. With a fine-point marker, draw a simple design of a boxy house in the center.

3. Thread your needle with no more than 20 inches of thread. Tie a large knot on the end.

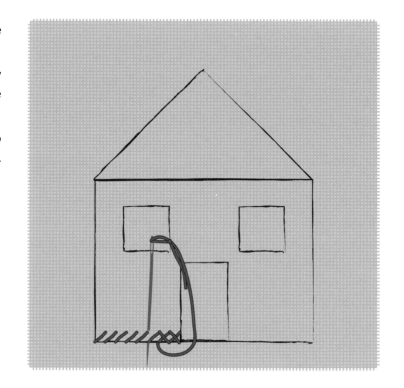

4. Starting from the back of the fabric, bring your needle up through the bottom left corner of the house. To keep your stitches uniform, use the grid of the burlap as your guide so the height and width of the X will always be the same. Count up three spaces in the burlap and over to the right three spaces. Put your needle in from the top and pull gently to create a diagonal line. Count straight down three spaces and bring your needle up. (It should be three spaces to the right of where you started.)

5. Continue across the bottom row of your house until you reach the door. End with your needle on top of the fabric on the bottom row.

6. The second part of the cross is easier. Lay your thread across the last diagonal and go down through the top stitch of the next one. Continue back across the row to form all the X's. Start the second row in the top left of the last X.

7. Once you finish the body of the house, change color and start on the door, windows, and roof. Be patient. Remember what George said: No problem is too big. All you need is 25 percent patience and 75 percent perseverance.

Work this stitch horizontally in two passes. First work half crosses from left to right. Then return, crossing the stitches from right to left.

Start a Rock Collection

"Rocks had an equal facination [*sic*] for me . . ."

If you are a budding naturalist like George and want to start a collection, rocks are a good place to begin. Your collection should reflect what you like. You can base it on color, shape, or geography, collecting from every place you visit.

ADULT SUPERVISION REQUIRED

YOU'LL NEED

- Empty egg carton
- Small paintbrush
- White paint
- Black felt-tipped marker
- Rock identification book or field guide
- Magnifying lens
- Notebook
- Geologist's hammer or carpenter's hammer (optional)
- Chisel (optional)
- Safety glasses

Look for rocks along creek beds, ditches, and areas where the soil has been moved or eroded away. Be careful and ask permission before you collect on someone else's property. Remember that it is usually illegal to collect in a national or state park. Check with a a park ranger first. Choose rocks that will fit into your egg carton.

When you get home, label your rocks. Lay them out on a covered surface. Brush off loose dirt or rub them with a damp rag. With a paintbrush, dab one small spot of white paint on each rock. The spot should be no bigger than the diameter of a pencil eraser. Let dry.

Write a number on each white spot with a black marker.

Use a field guide to identify each rock. (George did not have a book about rocks, but he examined his specimens carefully.) With the magnifying lens look for tiny flecks of minerals or fracture lines where the rock may have broken away from a larger boulder. Write down what you see in a notebook. Record the number, where you found the rock, the date you found it, and any identifying marks such as the color, lines, speckles, or shape.

To collect a sample from a rock that is too big to take home, use a geologist's hammer and chisel. The head of a geologist's hammer has two sides. One is blunt and the other is pointed. **Always wear safety glasses to protect your eyes from flying shards of rock.**

As your collection and interest grow, you can learn more about different rock classifications and build yourself a bigger box. George kept a few of his favorite childhood rocks all of his life. "I have some of the specimens in my collection now and consider them the choicest of the lot."

later, "but picked up the choicest ones and hid them in another place." In a few days, more rocks would be stacked against the house.

George observed everything, but plants won his heart. "Day after day I spent in the woods alone in order to collect my floral beauties and put them in my little garden I had hidden in the brush not far from the house." He dug up wild iris, blue chicory, white clover, purple coneflower, and Queen Anne's lace, and transplanted them in a patch of soil no bigger than his bed. "And many are the tears I have shed because I would break the roots of flowers of some of my pets while removing them from the ground." George learned each plant's needs, and when he didn't know a flower's name he made one up. They were his friends, and he talked to them—another habit he carried with him into adulthood.

"Look about you. Take hold of the things that are here. Let them talk to you. You learn to talk to them."
—George Washington Carver

His curiosity fueled experiments. What would happen if he planted red flowers next to blue flowers? Would they crossbreed and make purple flowers?

When neighbors heard about his skill with plants, they brought George their pots of wilted leaves, or invited him to their failing fields. More times than not, George nursed the plants back to life by changing the soil, altering the amount of water, or providing more sunlight. Even though he didn't know a plant's proper name he could diagnose diseases, identify mold, and spot insect damage. "Strange to say," he wrote, "all sorts of vegetation seemed to thrive under my touch until I was styled the plant doctor."

Although his flowers would eventually wilt, the paintings George created of them did not. He saw his first pieces of artwork in a neighbor's house, and from that day on he was an artist. With a careful eye for detail, he reproduced a flower's blooms on scraps of paper, bits of bark, smooth cut wood, any suitable surface in need of a little decoration. He mixed his paints as Susan mixed her fabric dyes, using the natural materials of the forest to create the red and yellow hues of his favorite flowers.

Locust Grove

One day George overheard a friend talking about Sunday school. That word—*school*—buzzed in his brain. He yearned to get the answers to all the questions that filled his head. That Sunday he tagged along with his friend to the Locust Grove Schoolhouse, which also served as a church. Methodists, Baptists, Presbyterians, and preachers of other denominations took turns riding into town to lead the white congregation. In Sunday school George listened to Bible stories and memorized verses. Afterward, he sat on the steps outside to listen to the church service for the grown-ups.

Unfamiliar tunes quickly became favorite hymns as his high-pitched voice rose in the air. George's faith grew, but that faith would be tested when Moses Carver enrolled George and Jim in school.

Like most rural schools at that time, the Locust Grove Schoolhouse consisted of a single room, with one teacher teaching students of all ages—but only white students. In 1865, Missouri lifted a ban on education for black children and required all school boards to provide a school for them if there were more than 20 African Americans between five and twenty years old living in their district. But George and Jim were likely the only black students in Diamond Grove, so there was no separate school for them.

Statue of young George holding a flower; George Washington Carver National Monument.
Photo by author

It must have been thrilling for George to walk to school on his first day. It was less than a mile away. He might have even run there because finally he was going to learn about the greater world around him. And in a way, he did—he learned about racial prejudice and exclusion. It is unclear how long the boys were allowed to stay at the Locust Grove Schoolhouse. Some folks remember it was only days before the parents of other students complained, and George and Jim were asked to leave. For a boy eager to learn, it must have been a frustrating lesson to discover that the doors open to him on Sundays were firmly closed to him the rest of the week.

Moses Carver, perhaps annoyed with the townsfolk, hired a tutor. Each afternoon, a man named Steven Slane arrived at the Carver farm to teach George. Slane brought George books, and years later Slane remembered George as "an exceptionally brilliant boy." It must have been thrilling for George to have something to read other than Susan's spelling book. But it soon became clear that Slane knew little more than his student. If George wanted more education, he would have to seek it elsewhere.

Mix Natural Paints

Being a young artist in the wilds of Missouri required a lot of imagination. In order for George to capture the beauty of his flowers, he had to create his paints first. For that, he turned to nature, using mashed berries, ground earth, and charcoal from the cold fireplace. He painted on pieces of smooth wood, clay pots, and scraps of paper he saved. Make your own paints and experiment with different colors as George did.

ADULT SUPERVISION REQUIRED

YOU'LL NEED
- Newspapers
- 4 small bowls
- Potato masher or fork
- ½ cup raspberries (or experiment with blackberries, mulberries, cherries, or blueberries)
- Strainer
- Flour
- 2 tablespoons turmeric powder
- Water
- Handful spinach
- Saucepan
- Small containers (recycled jelly jars or yogurt cartons)
- Paper
- Twigs
- Rock

1. Cover your work surface with newspaper. Set out your bowls to make three different paints.

   Red: With a potato masher or fork, mash ½ cup berries in a bowl. Strain the juice into a second bowl to extract as much liquid as you can. Discard the remaining berry bits. Stir flour a pinch at a time into the berry juice to thicken until it is the consistency of whole milk.

   Yellow: Place 2 tablespoons of turmeric in a bowl. Add 1 teaspoon of water at a time until the mixture has the proper thickness.

   Green: Place a handful of spinach in a small saucepan. Add ½ cup of water. Bring to a boil, stirring occasionally. Turn heat to low and simmer for 20 minutes. Mash with a potato masher. Let cool. Add flour to thicken.

2. What other natural materials could you use? Try crushed flower petals, paprika, or red pepper. Keep each paint you create in a separate container. Make a color swatch chart. Dab a bit of each paint on paper and label so you'll know what the dried colors look like.

3. Make a paintbrush with a twig the size of a pencil. Soak one end of the stick in water, then smash the tip of it with a rock to break up the fibers. Make one for each color.

A studio portrait of young George. The Carvers kept this picture after George left to find an education.
Tuskegee University Archives, Tuskegee University

2

AMONG STRANGERS

. . . wafted hither and thither, often among strangers . . . —George Washington Carver

Georg's thirst for an education must have been powerful, because one day he wrapped a change of clothes in a bandana, pocketed his favorite rocks, and said good-bye to Moses and Susan Carver, the only parents he had known for more than 10 years. "They encouraged me to secure knowledge helping me all they could but this was quite limited," George said. However, those early lessons set the foundation for the man he would become. From Moses he learned the value of hard work, resourcefulness,

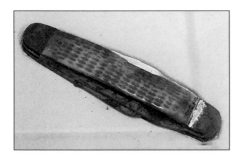

The pocketknife George took with him when he left home. *Photo by author*

and frugality, and from Susan he took all the necessary living skills of cooking, handiwork, and washing clothes.

Around that same time, Jim left the farm too. He may have gone to Fayetteville, Arkansas, for a while, but then returned to go to school with George. The Carvers were "perfectly willing for us to go where we could be educated the same as white children," said George. But it wouldn't be exactly the same. Schools for African Americans were a relatively new entity mandated by the government and segregated. The nearest "colored school" sat eight miles away in the town of Neosho.

George headed south, hiking through fields and forest, over hills and across creeks, probably growing more eager with each step. He had no idea what the school would be like, but he was more than ready to find out. By one account, it was growing dark as he stepped out of the woods and walked down Young Street in Neosho. In the dim light he could just make out the school, a small, plain one-story building. The windows on either side of the door were dark. It was clear that school was not in session. To the left of the school was a fine clapboard house surrounded by a picket fence. Behind it stood a barn similar to the one George had played in on the Carver farm. It must

Education During Reconstruction

In 1847 Missouri banned education for black persons. Slaveholders were afraid that education would inspire their slaves to rebel. But after the end of the Civil War and the abolishment of slavery in 1865, a period called Reconstruction began in which formerly enslaved Southerners gained many rights they had previously been denied. The 14th Amendment, ratified in 1868, gave African Americans citizenship. The 15th Amendment, ratified in 1870, gave black men the right to vote, and a Freedmen's Bureau helped organize badly needed education for more than three million people.

Towns were required to provide schools for all children regardless of color. Many school boards, however, ignored the mandate or underestimated how many school-aged children of color lived in their districts. Where "colored only" schools were created,

they usually received less funding than the "white schools." They were given old books, and little or no educational equipment like chalkboards, writing slates, or desks. Even the teachers were ill prepared. Ten years beyond slavery was hardly enough time to educate all the African American teachers who were needed to fill every schoolhouse. And few white teachers agreed to teach in the all-black schools. That left students learning from teachers who knew barely more than they did.

But the African American community understood that an education was the key to success. Literacy would allow them to understand contracts, negotiate terms of employment, open a business, lease or purchase a home, and keep in touch with family and friends.

What Is the Truth?

This question is often raised when discussing George's life. Just like his date of birth, his childhood story has many variations. He once gave this explanation for why there were so many versions about his childhood: "They don't realize that a poor colored orphan child, struggling to make a living, wafted hither and thither, often among strangers, not knowing where he would spend the night, or where he would get the next meal, have [sic] no time to think of important incidents in his life."

George's childhood may have been so traumatic that he truly did not remember what happened, and he also never expected to become so famous that dozens of journalists, biographers, and fans would want to know every detail. If George read an article about himself that had errors in it, he didn't correct them. In later years when he was lecturing, he kidded, "I like to hear myself introduced because I learn so many things about myself that I never knew." Much of what we know about his time in Neosho comes from anecdotes told by friends, neighbors, and acquaintances, and each, of course, had their own opinions.

have looked familiar and inviting, because George is said to have snuck inside to sleep.

The next morning an unfamiliar voice woke him. The startled woman had caramel skin and kind eyes. Her name was Mariah Watkins. George might have scrambled to explain his presence in her barn; if so, he must have done a good job, because Mariah invited him to stay with her and her husband, Andrew, in the fine clapboard house with the picket fence. Another biographer who interviewed George when he was an adult said that George went from house to house looking for a place to sleep until he found the Watkinses. Regardless of how he got there, the couple agreed that George could do chores around the house to pay for his room and board.

George sketched the Neosho school with the Watkinses' house on the left. Notice the arrow over the barn where he slept the first night.
Courtesy of the George Washington Carver National Monument

Mariah and Andrew Watkins

Mariah Watkins was a well-respected midwife who helped women during childbirth. Nearly every family in Neosho, black and white, knew her well. She began life in 1824, a slave in North Carolina, and may have learned midwifery from her slaveholder, a white doctor named Robert Scales who was possibly her father.

In 1872, Mariah married Andrew Watkins, who had once been enslaved in Texas. He worked at any job he could find, and may have been a blacksmith. In April 1874 they purchased a three-room house on Young Street in Neosho, making them one of the few African American families in town who owned property. They went on to purchase more than 40 acres. Although Mariah and Andrew Watkins never had children of their own, they often cared for children whose parents were traveling. One child she delivered remembered that "each summer Mariah would have a big birthday party for all of her 'kids,'" and they would fondly call them aunt and uncle.

Mariah Watkins.
Courtesy of the George Washington Carver National Monument

Living with the Watkinses gave George his first experience of town life. Neosho bustled with activity. Every morning men marched off to jobs at the machine shop, tobacco factory, brick kiln, or broom factory. Some headed out of town to one of several lead or zinc mines. Unlike the fresh earthy smells on the farm, the breeze brought in scents of hot ore from the local smelting furnace.

It was also the first time George had lived in a black community. More than 100 African Americans called Neosho home, and many of them lived in the same neighborhood. Every Sunday Mariah Watkins took George to the African American Methodist Episcopal Church several blocks away. The music there must have thrilled him, as he loved to sing. Watkins also gave him his first Bible, which he cherished all his life. "Indeed Mr. and Mrs. Watkins took me in just as one of the family."

Mariah Watkins was probably delighted to see how well George already knew the basic skills of washing, cooking, and sewing. Under her guidance, George learned even more, helping her with the laundry that she took in from townsfolk. He also kept the house, tended the garden, and milked the cow. With his keen interest in plants, George would have followed Watkins as she wandered the countryside looking for medicinal plants. Peeking over her shoulder, he'd watch as she carefully mixed her home remedies. When a woman went into labor, Watkins trotted off "in a narrow buggy, the seat barely holding her, hitched to a yellow, palomino-like pony."

Mariah Watkins was a stern taskmaster. One of George's friends, Calvin Jefferson, remembered her favorite phrase, "Toot, toot honey, no time for that," which meant, *Stop playing and get to work.* That was probably a good thing, because Jefferson remembered a time when he and George filled a tin can with water, lit a fire under it, and blew it up. But they didn't get into mischief all the time. Most of their games were typical street games where a can served as a ball, and the bushes were goalposts.

George had so much work that during recess from school he would jump the picket fence and do chores instead of play with the other kids. One friend remembered that he sometimes took a book with him and propped it up to read while scrubbing stains out of clothes. He may have done this in order to catch up to the students his own age, who had been in school longer.

They were used to the routine in the tiny school on Young Street. Once a "hall and parlor" home, it only had two rooms—the larger "hall," where the woodstove was located, and the smaller "parlor." In 1872 the Neosho school board bought the building to establish the first "colored" school in town. Inside the larger room, which measured 16 feet by 14 feet, were rows of "crude benches," where the students sat facing their teacher, Mr. Stephen Frost.

Thanks to a keen interest and desire to succeed, George quickly caught up to and surpassed his classmates. One girl, Amelia Thomas Richardson, recalled one day when Mr. Frost asked George to solve a problem on the chalkboard. "Oh it was a big problem on the board," she said. "He worked it and the teacher said it wasn't right."

Make Ginger Tea

One medicinal herb Mariah Watkins would have used was ginger root. Ginger works by calming the intestinal muscles. Aunt Mariah probably showed George how to settle an upset stomach with this tasty tea.

ADULT SUPERVISION REQUIRED

YOU'LL NEED

- Water
- Kettle
- Oven mitt
- Mug
- Knife
- Ginger root (you can substitute powdered ginger)
- Lemon
- Honey
- Spoon

Boil water in a kettle on the stove. Using an oven mitt, carefully pour into a mug. Cut two or three thin slices of ginger (or 1 teaspoon of powdered ginger) and drop into the hot water. Squeeze a bit of lemon juice into the mug. Add honey to taste, and stir.

The Carver Birthplace Association is working to restore the Neosho Schoolhouse. *Photo by author*

George erased his work and tried again, arriving at the same answer. Frustrated, George went home and told Mariah Watkins about his day. She suggested that George take the math problem to a high school teacher she knew, which he did.

The high school teacher checked George's work, wrote her name on the piece of paper, and declared it correct. George showed it to Mr. Frost the next day.

If this story is true, it is understandable if Mr. Frost made a mathematical error. Like most African American teachers at that time, he had little more education than his students. Cal Jefferson agreed that Mr. Frost "did not have much educational preparation, but he was an ideal teacher with the power to influence, inspire and impart knowledge and wisdom on what he knew."

Stephen S. Frost

Not much is known about Stephen Frost's past except that he was born in Tennessee around 1850. For a short time he lived in Springfield, Missouri, with the Baker family, whose daughter Emma was a schoolteacher. This is where he probably got his education, since there was only one black high school in the entire state, and the Lincoln Institute in Jefferson City was the only place that trained teachers. Stephen moved to Missouri, married Fannie Jefferson (Calvin Jefferson's older sister), and took Calvin in when his father died. With that same welcoming character and warm smile, Frost provided the stability and encouragement that his students needed when black communities were still figuring out how to thrive in a predominantly white society. "He was held in high regard and esteem by all the parents and citizens, both white and black in the city of Neosho," said Calvin. "About 95% of the students who completed work under him made good; that is they first had their education and became practical men and women." When a new school for African Americans was built in 1891, Frost became its first principal.

Mr. Frost also had a lot to focus on. His class consisted of 20 to 30 students of all ages in a cramped room. Imagine trying to learn math when the kindergartener next to you recites the ABC's. But it was in this atmosphere that George thrived. He even earned a "Reward of Merit" certificate for "perfect studies and good conduct" for the week of December 22, 1876. George knew, however, that this was only the beginning. "This," he said, "simply sharpened my apetite [sic] for more knowledge."

Moving to Kansas

One day in 1878, George heard that an African American family was moving west to Kansas. This was his chance. "I was anxious to go anywhere that I could get better school facilities." The Neosho school could only take him so far with basic reading, writing, and math, which he had already mastered. Even the other students noticed that "he was very smart and seemed really to know more than the teacher."

What Mariah and Andrew Watkins thought of this sudden move is unknown, but they may have approved of or even encouraged it. As the story goes, Mariah once sat George down and shared the story of a slave named Libby who taught Mariah how to read. Mariah then told George, "Learn all you can, then be like Libby. Go out in the world and give your learning back to our people."

The Carvers, on the other hand, did not approve when George went back to collect his "meager wardrobe." Years later he wrote, "When they heard from me I was cooking for a wealthy family in Ft Scott Kansas for my board, cloths [sic], and school privileges. Of course they were indignant and sent for me to come home at once, to die, as the family doctor had told them I would never live to see 21 years of age."

But at 13 years old, George was strong enough to trek the 75 miles northwest, walking or riding in a wagon, over the last rolling slopes of the Ozarks and into the flat Kansas plains. It took George and the family two weeks to make the journey.

George was part of a larger movement of black people from the South seeking better opportunities, and Fort Scott was a popular destination. Between 1870 and 1880, its African American population rose by 60 percent.

211 S. Judson Street

For whatever reason, George did not stay with the family he had traveled with. Instead he wandered

George earned this certificate for perfect studies and good conduct. *Tuskegee University Archives, Tuskegee University*

Exodusters

Reconstruction lasted until 1877, when federal troops pulled out of the former Confederate states. After it ended, Southern state and local governments adopted restrictive "black codes," which would become known as "Jim Crow" laws (a slur based on a white actor's caricature of a black man). Some laws prevented African Americans from owning property, or forced them to sign unfair labor contracts. Others were codes of behavior meant to keep African Americans isolated as much as possible. Any infraction could summon the cruelest punishment from racist groups like the Ku Klux Klan that terrorized and killed African Americans and anyone who supported them.

Kansas, on the other hand, seemed like the land of opportunity. Famous abolitionist John Brown had lived there. Encouraged by leaders like Benjamin "Paps" Singleton, who advertised the western movement, thousands of people fled to Kansas in pursuit of jobs and fairer treatment. Some settled in all-black towns like Dunlop and Nicodemus, while others took their chances homesteading.

Many African Americans seeking a better future out west were left on the banks of the Mississippi River, because ferrymen would not take them across on their way to Kansas.
Courtesy of the Library of Congress, LC-USZ62-26365

the dusty town looking for a job and a place to stay. In the African American section of Fort Scott, he noticed a blacksmith shop. He had helped Andrew with the horses a few times in Neosho; perhaps he hoped this smithy needed an extra hand.

When he knocked on the door of 211 S. Judson Street, the friendly face of Felix Payne greeted him. Known to be "free hearted," Payne took in George in exchange for chores around the house. He cooked and cleaned for the Payne family, washed clothes for guests at the Wilder House hotel, and may have worked at a grocery store too. When he earned enough money to attend school he enrolled in the Fort Scott Colored School, which was housed in the fort's old US Army hospital. The military had abandoned the property in 1873, leaving the building to the forces of the prairie, which threatened to overtake it.

Each morning, George hurried to the dilapidated building. It was still better than Mr. Frost's one-room schoolhouse. George devoured lessons in English, history, math, art, and science. The lesson that had the most impact, however, took place on the night of March 27, 1879. That night, 14-year-old George witnessed the horror of hatred and mob mentality.

The Lynching of Bill Howard

Earlier that day, everyone had been buzzing about the newest scandal. A black man by the name of Bill Howard had been accused of raping a 12-year-old white girl. George heard that after three days the white authorities finally tracked down

Howard, who had been hiding in an old coal mine. They hauled him back to the jailhouse to await prosecution.

At dusk, hundreds of angry white citizens swarmed the streets around the jail. George could hear the uproar from Judson Street. When asked to run an errand to the drugstore, George must have been terrified to walk out into the dark street, but he obeyed the order. That's when 30 masked white men stormed the jailhouse and hauled the accused out onto the street. They tied a rope around Howard's neck, "and amid thundering yells and shouts [he] was dragged by a hundred hands a distance of five blocks."

George stood frozen as the mob flooded down Judson Street. The hard-packed rocks and dirt shredded the man's clothes and skin. They beat Howard on the sidewalk, then picked up his limp body and hung him from a lamppost in the town square. The mob was rabid now. Despite calls for calm, some men pulled Howard down and burned his body "in a fire of dry goods boxes and coal oil."

With the stench of burning flesh in the air, George hurried back to the house, grabbed his few possessions, and fled Fort Scott. It was a gruesome lesson he would never forget. "As young as I was," he said 50 years later, "the horror haunted me and does even now."

Olathe

With no aim in mind other than to get as far away from the horror of the night, George fled north. He drifted for several weeks, and it was April by

the time he arrived in the town of Olathe, Kansas. Larger than Fort Scott, it had a thriving African American population of more than 600.

Ben and Lucy Seymour took him in. Lucy ran a laundry business and Ben dug wells. They lived with their 11-year-old son, Eddie, on Cherry Street between Poplar and Santa Fe, on the north side of town. George agreed to do chores in exchange for room and board. To earn money to pay for his schooling, he also shined shoes and cooked for the local barber, Mr. Jerry Johnson.

When he had earned enough, George enrolled in the newly established African American Old Rock School. It was the middle of the semester, but he managed to make a few friends.

Naturally quiet, he didn't usually play with the other children, but one day during recess he played marbles with Rashey B. Moten. Each time

The Fort Scott Colored School was located in the former Fort Scott military hospital. *Courtesy of the National Park Service / Fort Scott National Historic Site*

George's sketch of a leaf. *Tuskegee University Archives, Tuskegee University*

29

HAND-WASH A T-SHIRT

Washing clothes before the invention of the washing machine was a two-day affair. George soaked the clothes overnight to loosen soil. Then he scrubbed them on a washboard, wrung them out, and boiled them to kill any critters like lice. He then rinsed the clothes and hung them up to dry.

You can take a shortcut and still get a sense of what old-fashioned laundry was like.

YOU'LL NEED

- Large bowl
- Baking soda
- White vinegar
- Spoon
- T-shirt that you have outgrown
- Large washtub
- Washboard (or a 1-by-2-foot flat wooden board)

In the large bowl, measure out 2 tablespoons of baking soda. Add 2 tablespoons vinegar. The fizz is the reaction of the soda bicarbonate in the baking soda with the acetic acid in the vinegar. Stir into a paste.

Dampen the shirt, and then smear the paste onto the shirt using the spoon. Let sit for 30 minutes.

Fill a washtub halfway with warm water. Place a washboard in the tub. Vigorously rub the T-shirt up and down on the board, dunking it in the water occasionally.

Rinse shirt, wring out, and hang in the sun to dry. How long does it take? Now imagine if you had to wash for your whole family.

it was George's turn to shoot, his mind was elsewhere, usually examining the bushes and trees that lined the schoolyard. Rashey, eager to end the game before recess was over, had to nudge George to remind him of his turn. Rashey remembered that before they went back to class, George placed a leaf between the pages of a book for safekeeping.

In 1880 the Seymour family moved 175 miles west to Minneapolis, Kansas. George did not go with them. Instead, he wandered a short distance south to Paola, Kansas, where he found a room to let on East Miami Street with Willis and Delilah Moore, an African American couple with two children.

On June 14 a US census taker knocked on the door. Everyone in the household had to be

Washtub and washboard similar to the ones George purchased. *Photo by author*

accounted for. George gave his name and age, 15 years old, and said he worked in a laundry. He also attended the normal school, or high school, but did not complete the year. He may have missed the Seymours, because that summer he followed them to Minneapolis, Kansas.

Minneapolis

When George arrived in Minneapolis he saw few African American faces. Out of a population of 1,000, fewer than 30 were black. A predominantly white town might have given some African Americans pause if they had witnessed a lynching as George had, but he grew up in a white community, so this was a familiar setting to him. That summer, the small town buzzed with the construction noise coming from the site of the new opera house, and soon George would add another business to the growing community.

One of the first things he did was take out a loan for $54.45. That would have been enough money to buy an iron kettle, a washtub, washboard, soap, and other supplies for his laundry business. The only area that a poor African American teenager could set up such an enterprise was in the part of town commonly called Poverty Gulch. But that didn't bother George, who believed in the value of hard work rather than appearances or what people thought.

Poverty Gulch was not far from the Seymours' home on Second Street. Ben Seymour had traded in his pick and shovel for a hoe and plow, farming land just outside town. Lucy changed jobs as well and was now a nurse for Dr. James McHenry. George fell into the familiar pattern of working around the Seymour house for room and board, and washing clothes to pay for school. Occasionally, he ran errands for Dr. McHenry, who appreciated George's curiosity and intellect. McHenry loaned George his *McGuffey Reader* books and shared his interest in rocks.

Fifteen-year-old George spent most days at school, a two-story building with four rooms. Since Minneapolis had too few African American

Rock City—Did He or Didn't He?

When folks heard of George's rock collection, one of them was bound to have told him about the mysterious spherical boulders just south of town known as Rock City. Scattered across the plains like a giant's forgotten marbles sit sandstone concretions that were formed millions of years ago, when Kansas was under water. Water and wind carved away loose sandstone, revealing the unusual rocks that were held together with nature's concrete mix of sandstone and calcite. Bigger than a buggy, these round rocks would have captured George's imagination.

Although there is no evidence that George visited Rock City, how could a teen boy who was such a rock hound resist the urge to walk the three miles to see such a geological spectacle?

Rock City. *Courtesy of the Kansas Geological Survey*

students to warrant an all-black school, he attended lessons with mostly white students. His teacher taught Latin and Greek as well as history and science. Although he was still shy, George never felt that he needed to change in order to fit in. He continued to paint, crochet, and collect plant samples. He had grown a bit taller, but his voice had not changed. One classmate remembered, "He was quiet and did not mix with others in the playground. He would just stand and look around. He was very studious and very appreciative of his teachers." But George was also an integral part of the student body. On Fridays he played the

accordion or the harmonica for the school's afternoon program. He did make friends, including Chester Rarig, who invited George over for family meals.

July 29, 1883, was a Sunday, and George, freshly scrubbed and wearing a clean shirt and trousers, walked down Second Street with the Seymour family to the neat, white clapboard Presbyterian church. George had been attending services there for almost three years, but this day was special—he was officially becoming a member. It seems to have been an important moment for him, because in the membership book he didn't just write George Carver. For the first time on a public document, George gave himself a middle name. Maybe he thought it would give the occasion more weight, or as some historians say, it solved the problem of mixed-up mail with another George Carver. For whatever reason, George was now George Washington Carver. Throughout his life, George's signature rarely included his middle name. He only used the initial: George W. Carver.

A Visit Home

Sometime between 1881 and 1883, George traveled back to Diamond Grove to visit the Carvers and his brother Jim. Walking up to the Carver farm, George noticed startling changes. The old log cabin where he grew up was gone. In its place stood a fine two-story clapboard home Moses Carver had built in 1881.

Moses and Susan Carver, now in their seventies, were surprised at the strapping young man

Carver's clapboard house.
Photo by author

32

James Carver

James traveled on his own after studying for a short time at the Neosho school. He also worked on the Carver farm as a hired hand, but eventually James moved to Seneca, Missouri, where he either worked as a plasterer or for the railroad. In June 1883, at the age of 23, James came down with smallpox and died. "The sad news reached me . . . that James, my only brother had died," said Carver. "Being conscious as never before that I was left alone, I trusted God and pushed ahead."

James Carver. *Courtesy of the George Washington Carver National Monument*

who stood before them. On that trip, the Carvers gave him an old lamp, his mother's spinning wheel, and the bill of sale documenting the purchase of his mother Mary. It would be the last time he saw his brother.

Kansas City

George Washington Carver was growing up to be a fine young man. Physically, he was still thin, but he shot up in height, and at 19 years old had made a place for himself in the Minneapolis community. He attended church regularly. He was educated and well spoken. Townsfolk gave him all the laundry work he could handle, and he developed a keen business sense.

In 1884 Carver purchased two small plots of land for $100 and sold them nine months later for $500. It seemed that he had learned all he could in Minneapolis, so he said good-bye to the Seymours and headed to Kansas City, Missouri. Carver enrolled in a small business school where he learned shorthand and typing. He bought a typewriter and found a job as a stenographer and typist in the telegraph office at the Union Depot, Kansas City's main train station.

One morning Carver met Chester Rarig, his friend from Minneapolis, for breakfast at the Whittaker restaurant. They sat at the horseshoe-shaped counter. Before they could order, the waiter said to Rarig, "You can be served, but your friend cannot." Years later, Rarig recalled, "I was knocked silly. Having no thought of anything of the kind; but we both dismounted our stools and marched out as we had come in."

Rarig may have been surprised, but Carver was used to it, and he seemed embarrassed that his friend had to suffer the humiliation of racism as well. Standing on the sidewalk, Carver encouraged Rarig to go back in and eat. He assured his friend that he would find breakfast somewhere else. He never saw Rarig again.

Settlers cutting sod.
Nebraska State Historical Society

Carver had only been in Kansas City a few short months, but he was already dismayed and restless. Maybe it tugged at his heart to see so many people intently bustling through the Gothic arches of the train station on their way to their destinations. He needed to be somewhere he could continue his education. As he said years later, "The thirst for knowledge gained the mastery."

Highland to Homestead

Carver heard of a place called Highland University in Kansas. It was a small college of fewer than 200 students. The courses ranged from Latin and Hebrew to astronomy, math, and chemistry. It also was supportive of Presbyterian mission work. Eager to blend his work and his faith, Carver must have thought Highland would be a good place to continue his education. He applied by mail and was overjoyed to receive a quick acceptance.

The trip to Highland cost Carver almost all he had. When he got to the college his first thought was to call on the college president. "When the President saw I was colored he would not receive me," Carver said. Unbeknownst to him, Highland only admitted Native American students. The rejection hurt more than a punch in the stomach. It was a door slammed in his face, and completely unexpected. Carver left the campus unsure of his future. He only knew one thing. He couldn't afford to go back to Kansas City.

Carver had been on his own long enough to know that the only one he could count on was himself. His hard work would get him through.

He fell back on the skills he learned as a boy and set up another laundry service. He lodged with a white family named the Beelers and cooked and cleaned for them. The Beeler family ran a fruit farm south of town, and Carver would help prune trees and mend fences.

Some members of the Beeler family were land speculators. They created a town in the western part of Kansas and named it Beelerville (later shortened to Beeler). They sold business lots for $125 to $150, and residential property for $10 to $75. They built the Beeler Hotel and publicized the great opportunities to be had in Beelerville. Their advertisements seemed to have hit home for Carver. In 1886 he moved to Beelerville and took a job at the Beeler Hotel.

Homesteading on the Great Plains was back-breaking and tedious work. Long bouts of summer drought or a severe winter blizzard could drive even the most dedicated farmers back east. Many homesteads were left abandoned. It was one of these forgotten plots that Carver purchased on August 30, 1886. He was now a landowner of 160 acres. In order to officially own the property he would have to prove that he "shall reside upon and cultivate the land embraced in his homestead entry for a period of five years."

His first job was to build a house to live in. With no trees in sight, Carver created a sod house. With a special sod cutter, he dug long, deep furrows across the prairie, which he then cut into sod "bricks." Each brick measured roughly 12 by 24 by 4 inches. Stacking the bricks, Carver built a single-room home, 14 feet square. He coated the walls

A typical sod house.
Nebraska State Historical Society

with lime to prevent the soil from shifting, and formed a roof with a layer of boards, a layer of tar paper, and sod bricks on top.

During construction of his sod house, Carver lived with and worked for George Steeley, who co-owned the Gregg-Steeley Livestock Ranch. Carver cleaned, cooked, and acted as a general handyman, helping out with chores like building sod outbuildings around the ranch. What he learned on the ranch he applied to his own farm.

The winter was harsh. Temperatures rarely rose above zero, and the winds scoured the landscape. Livestock left outside grew thin and wandered off in storms to die miles from home. Carver was glad he had missed the blizzard the year before, which devastated the area and left many frozen to death in their sod houses.

BUILD A SODDY

The pioneers who settled on the prairie had to be creative when it came to building a home. Prairie grass grew as far as the eye could see, so that became their building material. A settler cut the grass, and then cut the sod in long strips four to eight inches deep and a foot wide. The strips were cut into blocks two feet long. They stacked the blocks grass side down to build the walls. Log planks formed a roof with sod placed on top.

Try your hand at stacking bricks by building your own edible sod house.

ADULT SUPERVISION REQUIRED

YOU'LL NEED

- Small bowl
- Green food coloring
- 2 cups shredded coconut
- Large spoon
- 1 flat baking pan or jelly roll pan
- Cooking spray or oil
- Large saucepan
- 6 tablespoons butter
- 2 packages of marshmallows, 10 ounces each
- 9 cups Cocoa Krispies
- Spatula
- Knife
- Baking sheet or sturdy cardboard
- 6–8 whole graham crackers

1. In a small bowl stir three to four drops of green food coloring into 2 cups of shredded coconut. Mix until all the coconut is green. This will be your grass. Set aside.

2. Grease a jelly roll pan or large flat baking pan with cooking spray or oil. Set aside.

3. In a large saucepan, melt 6 tablespoons butter on low heat. Stir in the marshmallows until melted. Add Cocoa Krispies 1 cup at a time until thoroughly mixed.

4. Transfer the mixture and press into the pan with a greased spatula. It should be thinner than typical marshmallow treats. Sprinkle the coconut flakes over the mixture. Press lightly so they stick. Cool in the refrigerator.

5. Cut rows 1 inch wide. Then cut the rows into 2-inch blocks.

6. On a clean baking sheet or firm piece of cardboard, build a sod house. Your soddy should be no bigger than 10 by 6 inches. Lay your bricks grass side down as the pioneers did. Leave a space for a door. As you stack each layer (five or six), overlap the bricks to make the walls stronger.

7. Lay a quarter of a graham cracker over the top of your window and door.

Place whole graham crackers on top, forming a flat roof. The remaining sod blocks go on top, grass side up. Take a peek inside and imagine what life would be like living in a soddy.

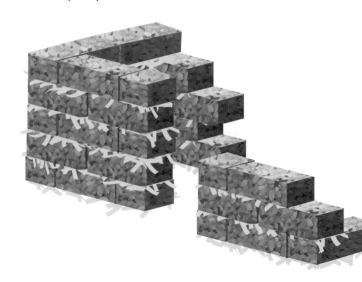

By April 1887, Carver, who was now 21 years old, moved into his finished soddy. No longer would he have to board with another family or clean someone else's house. His home belonged to him. At times it must have reminded him of the log cabin he grew up in—small and dark—and he furnished it just as simply with a cookstove, a bed, a table and chairs, and a small cupboard.

The life of a prairie farmer was not a leisurely one. Each day Carver had to fetch water from a creek on Steeley's property because not a single inch of his 160 acres had a source of water on it. Every attempt to dig a well came up dry. Without any trees to cut down, Carver used the dried disks of buffalo dung that peppered the prairie as fuel for the cookstove. He kept his pile of chips stacked high for the coming winter.

Over the next year, using only a spade hoe and his strong back, Carver turned over 17 acres of land. Under the Kansas sun, he planted 10 acres of corn and sorghum (a tall grain similar to corn that can be ground into flour or boiled down to make a sweet syrup). Each morning he gathered eggs from 10 chickens and weeded a vegetable garden. To improve his land, he planted 800 forest trees and 50 fruit trees such as mulberry, apricot, and plum.

The landscape he lived in continued to fascinate him. Carver wandered west, and for the first time he saw exotic cactus and yucca plants. He would carry home any interesting rocks or plants he saw over the course of the day. He kept his rock collection at his soddy, but the 500 plants he tended grew in a makeshift greenhouse at Steeley's place.

On June 21, 1888, Carver went to the County Clerk's office to "prove up" by providing evidence of his homesteading efforts. His friend Steeley testified on his behalf. "I have seen him most every week," Steeley said, "some weeks every day, and know he has acted in good faith under his circumstances." Four days later Carver took out a loan for $300. Instead of waiting five years to be the legal landowner, he purchased the land outright for $200.

Although he lived alone, Carver's life was not solitary. He had many friends, including another African American homesteader named Bird Gee, who later opened a market in town. Clara Duncan, an artist, also lived in town and gave Carver art lessons. More friendships developed with the local newspaper editor, a county official, and several other white men. In a letter he wrote to O. L. Lennen, Carver remembered his time in Ness County and appreciated that folks "were able to look into the future of a struggling young Negro boy and discern that there was something in him worthy of a chance in life like other folks."

On cold winter evenings Carver walked under a star-filled sky to Steeley's place to play music. Steeley played the violin, Gregg played the guitar, and Beeler played the coronet. Carver rounded out the quartet with the accordion, harmonica, guitar, or violin.

Everyone who met Carver seemed to be impressed with his wide-ranging knowledge.

"When I was in the presence of that young man," said one Ness County citizen, "I was humiliated by my own inadequacy of knowledge, compared to his." The *Ness County News* featured Carver in its March 31, 1888, edition: "He is a pleasant and intelligent man to talk with, and were it not for his dusky skin—no fault of his—he might occupy a different sphere to which his ability would otherwise entitle him."

Carver must have felt the same way. In his heart he knew he could do and be so much more than what was then considered acceptable for a black man. He needed to find that "different sphere" where he could elevate himself as well as people's expectations of all African Americans. Shortly after that article appeared, Carver took the remaining $100 of his loan and left his farm.

George W. Carver the artist.
Courtesy of the George Washington Carver National Monument

3

A REAL HUMAN BEING

When you can do the common things in life in an uncommon way, you will command attention of the world. —George Washington Carver

In early autumn of 1888, while the weather was still warm, Carver headed north. After weeks of meandering through Nebraska and into Iowa, he settled in the small town of Winterset, 35 miles from Des Moines. Perhaps he was tired of traveling, or perhaps there was something about Winterset that felt right. It was a predominantly white community, and although Carver did not know a soul, it was a familiar setting. With his excellent cooking and cleaning skills, he had no trouble getting a job at the

St. Nicholas Hotel on the corner of Jefferson and Second Street. "I cooked at this hotel for some time; then opened a laundry for myself," he said. "I ran this laundry for one year."

One Sunday, Carver found a welcoming church and sat in the back pew. Heads must have turned at the sight of his tall slender figure. He no longer looked like a boy. The relentless work on his homestead had turned him in to a strong man of about 24 years old.

At the front of the church a woman with a fine voice led the choir. Carver sang along with the familiar hymns and prayed with the rest of the congregation. "The next day," he said, "a handsome man called for me at the hotel, and said his wife wanted to see me." The man, whose name was Dr. John Milholland, was a respected physician in town, and his wife was Helen. Unsure of what Mrs. Milholland could possibly want, George agreed to meet her.

After work Carver walked up the steps of the "splendid residence." When she appeared at the door, he recognized her right away. She was the woman who led the church choir. The attraction was mutual, for it was George's fine tenor voice that made Mrs. Milholland seek *him* out. They chatted for a bit, and then Mrs. Milholland asked him to sing. "I had to sing quite a number of pieces for her and agreed to come to her house at least once a week." This middle-aged prosperous white woman and poor black young man had much in common: their Christian faith, music, and art. Mrs. Milholland enjoyed painting, and marveled at Carver's ability to bring his canvases to life.

Each time they'd meet, Carver would tell her about his day—of his long morning walks, whose clothes he had washed, what he cooked for lunch at the hotel, his newest painting, and, of course, music. His energy and busy schedule impressed and amused Mrs. Milholland. She once told him, "Whoever heard of any one person doing half so many things."

The Milholland family.
Courtesy of the George Washington Carver National Monument

One day, Mrs. Milholland suggested that Carver go to college. It had been more than three years since the Highland University incident, and although the sting of that rejection had faded, it was still a sore subject. After that conversation, Carver avoided Mrs. Milholland. After several days, she grew worried and "sent one of the girls down to the house . . . to see what was the matter." As Carver explained years later, "It was my decision with reference to college that was troubling me." Mrs. Milholland had put the idea into his head, but he could not do anything about it. It pained him to think how long it would take for him to earn enough money for tuition, travel, and room and board. And in the back of his mind, he must have been wondering if it would be just a waste of time again.

While ironing a shirt a few days later, "feeling very much depressed," a voice in his head asked, "Why *don't* you go to college?" "I had no money, was already in debt, only two months before school opened, and I just could not do it." Forgetting about the hot iron searing a hole into the shirt, Carver argued with himself until finally he made up his mind. "I turned entirely around and said to this voice, 'I will.'"

When he told Mrs. Milholland about his decision she was delighted. Because of his obvious talent for painting, she suggested that Carver apply to the art school at Simpson College 25 miles from Winterset. It took him a year to raise enough money to pay for tuition. Fall semester cost $12, which to him meant raw red hands from long hours of scrubbing laundry and wringing it dry.

Simpson College

On September 9, 1890, Carver became a college student. At about 26 years old, he was older than the average freshman and was the only African American on campus. He likely turned a few heads, which he greeted with smiles and a polite nod. Indianola, where Simpson was located, was slightly larger than Winterset and would eventually prove to be even friendlier, but it would take some time.

Like all first-year students, his initial task was to find a place to live. At the time, female students lived in dormitories, but male students roomed off campus with local families. Carver went from house to house, but no one would take him in.

Simpson College. *Courtesy of the Simpson College Archives*

Worries gnawed at him. What would it take to make these people like him? He was about to give up when the college president intervened. He found him an abandoned shack a block away from school. It was far from ideal, and certainly not equal to the kind of homes other students enjoyed, but to Carver it was just enough.

To furnish his home, Carver asked shopkeepers for empty crates to serve as a table and chairs. He went to the town dump and dragged back a wrecked woodstove that he could fix. Then he took a loan out from the bank and purchased two washtubs and a boiler. His shack was not the cozy family environment that the white students were given, but it allowed him the room to set up his laundry service.

By the time he paid his school fees, Carver was left with ten cents, just enough to buy five cents' worth of corn meal and five cents' worth of beef fat, called suet. "I lived on these two things a whole week," he said. "It took that long for the people to learn that I wanted clothes to wash."

Carver may have scrubbed other people's clothes each morning and night, but during the day he was a dedicated college student. He wore a suit to class like all the other male students, although his cuffs were frayed and his pants too short. But his shirts sparkled, and he always wore a flower in his lapel.

Because of Carver's spotty education in Neosho, Fort Scott, and Minneapolis, he had to take classes in grammar, math, and writing. But soon he was able to add voice and piano lessons, which he paid for with paintings.

At first, the art teacher, a young woman named Etta Budd, disliked the idea of having Carver in her art program. The color of his skin didn't worry her. But did he have talent? As soon as she saw his fine color work and controlled brushstrokes, she welcomed him to her class.

The first day of art class, Carver, dressed in a dark suit, climbed the three flights of stairs to the top of the Scientific and Normal Hall. The art room's tall windows let in an abundance of sunshine to work by, and the high ceilings allowed plenty of room on the walls for a gallery of framed portraits and landscapes. Most of the students were young women who may have raised an eyebrow when he walked in. But there, set before an easel, was a seat waiting just for him.

Under Miss Budd's instruction, Carver studied master painters and worked on brushstrokes. He learned to layer colors to create just the right effect. One painting he worked on from memory; a large canvas of "an [original] design of the cactus and yucca." For Carver, painting was an extension of his spiritual life. "I have wanted my painting of flowers to speak . . . to the beholder," he said, "and lift their souls beyond the sordid things of life, and give them a glimpse of the creator who shapes and fashions all of our destinations."

It is around this time at Simpson College that Carver began to feel that God had a plan for him. On April 8, 1890, he wrote to Mrs. Milholland,

(above) **The Budd family, with Etta in front.** *Iowa State College Archives*

(left) **Carver in art class.** *Tuskegee University Archives, Tuskegee University*

"I am taking better care of myself than I have, I realize that God has a great work for me to do and consequently I must be very careful of my health." This sense of a mission may have blossomed out of all of the religious activities he participated in. He had joined the Bible study group on campus, the Young Men's Christian Association (YMCA), and the local African Methodist Church in town. But it was also the acceptance he felt on campus that made him feel at home. One classmate remembered that, "we saw so much beyond the color that we soon ceased to sense it at all."

When students brought their laundry to Carver's home, he'd unselfconsciously offer them a crate to sit on, and they would stay and chat. One day he came home to find his crates gone. He walked in on a room full of new furniture. All of his friends had taken up a collection and purchased him a table, chairs, and a bed. It must have been difficult for Carver to accept such an extravagant gift. He prided himself on being self-sufficient and working for all that he had. He never took handouts. But the boys must have felt that his friendship was payment enough. Years later Carver wrote, "They made me believe I was a real human being."

Mrs. Liston

As Carver delivered packages of freshly pressed shirts and blouses, he met many of his neighbors too. Occasionally, he stopped in Liston's Book Store on the north side of the town square. He and the shopkeepers, Mrs. Sophia Liston and her husband, William, talked about art and life as Carver paged through new titles. When he needed a place to study, Mrs. Liston invited him to their home, where the bay window served as a quiet spot for him to do his homework. For many years Carver and Mrs. Liston kept in touch through letters. She would sign her letters "Your mother."

The "dinkey" steam train.
*Farwell T. Brown Photographic Archive,
Ames Public Library*

One of the topics Carver and Mrs. Liston might have discussed was his career as an artist. Miss Budd was concerned that a black man could not earn a living in the art world. Carver couldn't think of doing anything else. He was born to be a painter. But Budd suggested that he study agriculture. In class she had witnessed his keen artistic eye for plant details, but most painters did not know the names of the flowers that they drew, or where they grew, or how they thrived. She recognized that Carver's real talent was botany, the study of plants. Budd knew a bit about botany because her father, Joseph L. Budd, was a professor at the agricultural college at Ames, Iowa.

Carver's faith and everything he had witnessed had been leading him to choose a career that would be useful to other African Americans. Could he do that through his art? Maybe. But the more he thought about it, the more he realized that he could help more people by studying agriculture, or farming. In the fall of 1891, Carver transferred to Iowa Agricultural College (IAC).

A Chilly Welcome

Carver had spent half his life moving from place to place, and it should have been an easy transition for him to go to IAC, but Simpson had become his home. He was not only leaving dear friends, he was turning his back on the art that he loved. Carver needed reassurance that he was doing the right thing in pursuing a career that would help lift up all African Americans.

Iowa and the Morrill Act

When Carver arrived at IAC it already was a top school for agricultural education and research. Because farming was an integral part of the economy, the government was getting increasingly involved as farming grew more and more into a scientific endeavor. In 1862 Congress passed the Morrill Act, which allowed states to create agricultural and technical colleges from the sale of public lands. These schools became known as land-grant colleges, and Iowa was the first.

When he arrived in Ames, Carver found a city that rarely encountered people who looked like him. Once again, he was breaking new ground as the first black student out of 425 attending IAC. According to one classmate, Carver was also the only African American out of 1,250 town residents. Now about 27 years old, he was used to the glares and surprised looks as he headed toward campus. If he had five cents to spare he could have ridden the dinkey, a small steam engine that ran between Ames and the college. But chances are Carver hiked several miles across a creek, through woods, and up a hill to a stately cluster of stone buildings. Walking across campus, a group of boys shouted at him. They were not words of welcome.

Living arrangements at IAC were similar to Simpson College. As Carver searched for a place to stay, he also got the same reaction. One professor tried to help but said that people "liked Mr. Carver well enough but owing to the fact that he was a colored boy they all said they would not like to have him in the house." Finally, the director of the agricultural department let Carver live in an empty office in North Hall. In return, Carver became the unofficial janitor cleaning the building and doing minor repairs. That August, he wrote to the Milholland family and said, "I as yet do not like it as well here as I do at S[impson] . . . but the Lord helping me I will do the best I can."

At mealtime, Carver entered the dining hall with all the other students. Everyone found a seat at one of dozens of small tables neatly set with a white tablecloth and silverware. But when the manager of the dining hall spied Carver, he hurriedly directed him down the stairs to eat in the basement. Carver did what he was told. It wasn't the first time he'd been segregated, and it wouldn't be the last. But he longed for recognition of who he was inside, and not what he looked like on the outside. To get his fears and worries off his chest, he wrote about the incident in a letter to Mrs. Liston.

A few days later, Carver was stunned to see Mrs. Liston in her best dress and hat marching across campus to greet him. She wanted a tour, so Carver showed her his classes, his room, and at mealtime they ate in the basement together. The dining hall manager must have been mortified to watch as Mrs. Liston lifted her voluminous skirts and carefully stepped down the narrow stairs to lunch because "the next day everything was different, the ice was broken, and from that [day] on, things went very much easier."

Carver and the dairy class.
Iowa State College Archives

48

Learning About Agriculture

The agricultural program involved a lot more than mastering how to plow, plant, and harvest. Carver took classes in history, algebra, elocution (public speaking), entomology (the study of insects), chemistry, bacteriology, pathology (the study of disease), botany (the study of plants, their anatomy, and how and where they grow), and horticulture (the study of plants and how people cultivate and use them). He excelled at everything. Well, not so much at math. His heart wasn't in it. But he loved the hands-on classes with plants.

The teachers in the agricultural department were the best in the country. His horticulture teacher was Joseph Budd. Professor Budd had heard from his daughter Etta all about Carver and his skill with plants. Carver spent many hours in the greenhouse learning the proper way to cross-breed flowers to get bigger blooms or make them disease resistant. It must have been gratifying to think about the many times he had fumbled with these concepts on his own as a child, and here he was years later learning the science behind them.

Harry C. Wallace taught soil conservation. Carver called him "a master of soils." Wallace had been a farmer before he was a professor, and he believed that a farmer "must understand his soil, and the laws of nature operating therein. He must understand the plants which he grows, and the livestock which convert the plants to meat."

Because Carver was much older than the average student, he easily made friends with professors as well as students. They all welcomed him

FORM A WELCOMING COMMITTEE

As soon as Mrs. Liston heard about Carver's chilly reception at IAC, she did not hesitate to appear on campus in a show of solidarity for him. She wouldn't have needed to if his classmates had been more welcoming. It is not fun being the new kid in school, especially if you look different, as Carver did. Put yourself in the new kid's shoes. You are surrounded by strangers in a strange place. You don't know the schedule or what is expected of you. You just wish someone would say hello.

Be that someone. Organize a Welcoming Committee in your school, a group of students who will mobilize when a new student arrives. Create a welcome packet with important information that kids at your school should know (like what the best meal is in the cafeteria). Pledge to learn new students' names and tell them yours, say "Hi" every time you see them, introduce them to others, and make sure they never sit alone in the cafeteria.

into their homes and invited him to Sunday meals. James Wilson, for example, was the director of the school's experiment station. He and Carver spent many hours in a weekly Bible study class. Carver may have been an orphan, but he was considered family by many of his teachers. Wallace's son, six-year-old Henry A. Wallace, followed Carver around like a puppy. When Carver went on his nature walks, Henry A. tagged along. Carver pointed out every species of shrub, bug, and slug.

One day, Carver and Henry A. quietly watched as bees buzzed among the wildflowers. When a bee landed on a petal to collect nectar, bright yellow pollen stuck to the bee's legs. When it flew to another flower, some of the pollen dropped off, pollinating it. Before the bee moved on, more pollen clung to its legs. Years later Henry A. remembered, "It was he [Carver] who first introduced me to the mysteries of plant fertilization."

Carver spent most of his time with Professor Louis Pammel, one of the greatest botanists in the country. He must have felt like Professor Pammel read his mind. Carver had always felt a strong connection to all living things. So did Pammel. They both witnessed that relationship between plants and other animals every time they hiked in the woods. Carver saw it in the decay of a felled tree nurturing mushrooms and ferns, and he noticed how certain birds flocked together according to which trees were in fruit. Today we call these complex relationships *ecosystems* and the study of them *ecology*. But that was a new idea when Carver was in college, and Pammel was an early supporter. His book *Flower Ecology* was the first English-language text with the word *ecology* in the title.

Pammel opened Carver's eyes to the idea of invasive species, too, and people's role in introducing them to a landscape. Carver had seen it himself as he hiked across the country, noticing how thickly weeds and wildflowers sprouted up along roads and railroad tracks. Certain plants "followed" man's well-traveled routes. With the arrival of new plants came new predators. For the first time farmers and scientists were seeing harmful species like the boll weevil and wheat rust threatening America's crops.

Botanist Louis Pammel.
Iowa State College Archives

BE A BEE

Pollination is one way that plants reproduce. It is the transfer of pollen from the stamen, the male part of the plant, to the female part, called the pistil. While bees and other insects are busy feeding on a flower's nectar, pollen sticks to their legs. The insects move the pollen from one flower to another as they continue feeding. If the pollen falls into the same flower or another flower on the same plant, the plant has self-pollinated. If the bee transfers the pollen to a flower on another plant, these plants have cross-pollinated.

YOU'LL NEED

- 2 flowering plants of the same type in bloom (the easiest flowers to work with are lilies, hibiscus, or petunias)
- Small paintbrush or cotton swab

1. Examine a flower on one of your plants carefully. Identify its parts.

   Petal—the colorful modified leaves that surround the reproductive parts of a plant.

   Pistil—the female part of the plant, located in the center of the flower. It is made up of the ovary at the base, the style or stalk that rises from the ovary, and the stigma at the top of the style, which acts as a landing pad for the pollen.

   Stamen—the male part of the plant, made up of several hairlike filaments that surround the pistil. Each filament has a pollen-filled anther at the top.

2. With a small paintbrush or cotton swab gently rub the pollen off the anthers. What color is the pollen? Rub the pollen on the stigma of the same flower. Repeat with a flower on the second plant. Now the plants will continue their life cycles creating seeds that can be planted next year.

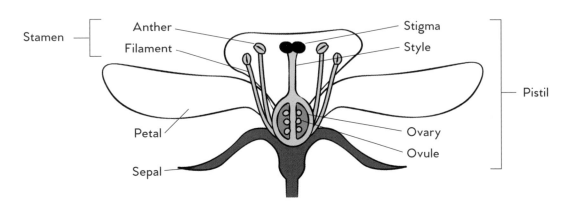

Stamen — Anther / Filament

Petal

Sepal

Stigma / Style

Pistil

Ovary / Ovule

(left) Carver in later years carrying his botanist's vasculum. *Tuskegee University Archives, Tuskegee University*

(right) Herbarium specimen.
Photo by author

Carver's early morning nature walks took on academic seriousness. He acquired a vasculum, a special carrying container for collecting plant specimens. Now instead of looking like a hobo collecting weeds, he looked like a professional botanist. When he found a new species he snipped a sprig off the plant and slipped it into his container where it would not get crushed as he hiked along.

Make a Botanist's Vasculum

ADULT SUPERVISION REQUIRED

YOU'LL NEED

- Empty carton from plastic wrap, foil wrap, or parchment paper
- Adult helper
- Tape
- Newspapers
- Acrylic paint
- Paintbrush
- Inch-wide grosgrain ribbon (1 to 1½ yards)
- Scissors
- 2 brad fasteners
- Velcro fasteners

1. Have an adult carefully remove the sharp, serrated cutting strip from a long plastic wrap carton. Repair any rips with tape.

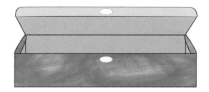

2. Protect your work surface with newspaper. Then paint the carton your favorite color. Let dry.

3. Measure out and cut a length of ribbon so that your vasculum will hang comfortably from your shoulder or across your chest. Add 4 inches to account for the 2-inch overlap on each end of the carton.

4. With a brad, affix one end of the ribbon to one end of the carton. Repeat on the other side.

5. Find where the flap overlaps with the side of the container. Mark the middle point. Stick one piece of the Velcro on the front, and the second piece inside the flap. Trim any excess.

6. Take your new botany case when you collect plants for the next activity: making your own botany collection.

Make Your Own Herbarium

YOU'LL NEED

- Plant identification guidebook
- Notebook and pencil
- Scissors
- Paper towels or newspaper
- Vasculum (see page 53)
- Lots of books or other heavy objects
- Toothpick
- White glue
- Thick paper (card stock)
- Pen

Before you collect your first specimen, ask permission. Many parks and nature preserves do not allow collecting. Using the guidebook, identify the flower or plant. (Before you handle any plant, make sure it is not poison ivy or poison oak, or another plant that isn't safe to handle.) Record the name of the plant, date, and location in your notebook. Cut the plant low on the stem to preserve several rows of leaves and flower. Dampen a paper towel and wrap it around the cut end of the plant. Place in your vasculum to bring home.

1. Prepare each flower. On two or three sheets of paper toweling or newspapers, arrange the plant so that the leaves are flat and the flower is facing up. Cover with two more paper towels.

2. Place several heavy books on top to flatten the plant. You can stack several specimens with one or two books in between each plant. Leave undisturbed for at least a week.

3. Unstack the books. Discard the paper towels to reveal your herbarium specimens. Carefully lift the plant and use a toothpick to dot white glue along the back of the plant, under a leaf, and along the flower. Lay the flower on thick paper, pressing gently.

4. Every herbarium specimen needs a label. In the bottom right corner of the paper, record this information.

   Specimen #

   Date Collected:

   Name:

   Location/Habitat:

   Flower Color:

   Collected by:

   Notes:

Optional: Keep your specimens in a shirt box, or create a folder for them out of cardboard.

When he got back to college, Carver prepared his specimens by pressing and drying them so he could mount the dried flower on a sheet of paper to be added to the herbarium, a botany research collection.

Extracurricular Activities

Carver seemed to embrace every opportunity available to him. He joined the art club, the German club, and a debating club called the Welch Eclectic Society. He was a fierce yet compassionate competitor too. The Welch Eclectic Society sponsored an oratory contest where students were judged as they gave a speech. Carver and his friend Truman Penney entered. The night before the contest, he heard a knock on his door. It was Penney—he was worried about his speech. Carver listened while Penney practiced and assured him that he would do just fine.

The next day at the competition, Carver watched as Penney stood before the podium, shaking. Carver smiled, which Penney appreciated. Then it was Carver's turn. Even with his unusually high-pitched voice, he captivated the judges and won first prize. Years later when the two friends met again, Penney still remembered Carver's kindness.

In the little spare time he had, Carver played bit parts in plays and gave music lessons to friends. All the men on campus had to participate in the school's military division. Carver earned the rank

(left) **Carver and the Welch Eclectic Society.** *Iowa State College Archives*

(below) **Carver as Quartermaster.** *Iowa State College Archives*

GIVE A SPEECH

Oratory is a speech that informs the audience about a particular topic. It's a form of debate meant to persuade or move the listener. Carver would have learned how to give a great speech by memorizing one given by a great speaker. You can too. Choose a speech like the Gettysburg Address by Abraham Lincoln, or check out the speeches of Frederick Douglass or Martin Luther King Jr. Read the text, write out the text, and recite it aloud until you have it memorized. Practice your presentation. Feel the words and what they mean. Speak clearly, and alter your tone of voice to emphasize key points. Don't forget eye contact. Look at your audience and make a connection. Learn other oratory tips from the National Speech and Debate Association at www.speechanddebate.org.

of captain. When the football team needed a trainer to rub their sore muscles, Carver took the job. One player remembered that he had "a magic touch in those long fingers." Carver wrote poems for the school newspaper and was active in the YMCA.

And in all these endeavors he made friends. Once people were willing to see beyond their prejudices they naturally gravitated toward Carver's kind and gentle manner. By his second year, his friends were so true that for the second time in his life he was "kidnapped"—this time for his own good.

The Art Show

Carver heard about an upcoming art show and was encouraged to submit some of his paintings. But the show was more than 100 miles away in Cedar Rapids. There was no way he could afford the trip. His friends thought otherwise.

The day after Christmas, 1892, Carver looked out the window at the white snowy world and dressed in his shabby work clothes and threadbare coat. One of his professors had hired him to clean house after a holiday party. He never said no to a chance to earn extra money. Outside, Carver pulled his thin coat tighter around himself and began the walk into town. A sleigh pulled up with several friendly faces peeking from beneath woolly hats. In a puff of breath, the driver offered him a lift.

As the horse jingled on, Carver got caught up in talking. Several minutes passed before he realized they were nowhere near the professor's house—they were headed downtown. The sleigh finally pulled up in front of a clothing shop for men. The friends escorted a protesting Carver inside. Between sputters of objection, they managed to get Carver into a brand-new suit that Professor Pammel had arranged to buy for him. They completed the outfit with new underwear, coat, gloves, and hat, everything he would need for a chilly train ride to Cedar Rapids. Professor Wilson handed him a ticket, along with four of Carver's best paintings that had been bundled in stiff paper to protect them on the trip.

Carver, years later, with his prizewinning painting *Yucca gloriosa*. *Tuskegee University Archives, Tuskegee University*

Leaders in Agriculture

Iowa Agricultural College led in agricultural education, but also in staffing the federal government. James G. Wilson, the "master of soils" became US secretary of agriculture in the cabinets of William McKinley, Theodore Roosevelt, and William H. Taft. Henry C. Wallace became secretary of agriculture for Warren G. Harding. And Henry A. Wallace, who at six years old had followed Carver around, grew up to become secretary of agriculture and, for a short time, served as 33rd vice president of the United States under Franklin D. Roosevelt.

As a child, Henry A. Wallace hiked with Carver. He grew up to be USDA secretary and a US vice president.
Iowa State College Archives

57

When Carver arrived at the art show, he naturally pitched in to help set up. The judges awarded all his paintings with ribbons, and chose *Yucca gloriosa*, the large canvas he created at Simpson, to represent Iowa in the 1893 World's Columbian Exposition in Chicago.

"The Great Whole"

Everything was coming together for Carver. He was as happy at IAC as he had been at Simpson, maybe more so. He made many friends and several families had "adopted" him. His reputation as a botanist and horticulturist grew. The Iowa State Horticultural Society invited him to speak about a paper he wrote on the cactus, a plant he admitted was prickly and hated by many people. But, he added, the cactus was important to the environment.

> **"Nature does not expend its forces upon waste material."**
> **—George Washington Carver**

If nature created it, it must have a purpose. Carver was good at finding that purpose. He took notes on the back of discarded wrapping paper and wrote with teeny pencil stubs others had thrown away. For snacks, he collected edible weeds and cooked them in his room. For close to 20 years he had survived alone making do with what nature provided.

In that speech he also said, "Each created thing is an indispensable factor in the great whole, and one in which no other factor will fit exactly as well." Carver was talking about the cactus, but in many ways he felt that way about people too. Everyone had a role to play in the world and like an ecosystem, they had to work together. The vision that would eventually direct the rest of his life's work was becoming clearer.

Carver's graduation portrait. *Iowa State College Archives*

"Professor" Carver

On November 13, 1894, Carver became the first African American to graduate from IAC. The caption under his picture in the yearbook reads, "Gifted with an intense love of nature." Without hesitation, Carver enrolled in graduate school. He was also hired as assistant botanist in the experiment station. Carver became the first African American teacher at Iowa and must have felt proud of the achievement. Even so, he still felt the sting of racism. Usually it happened at the beginning of the year when freshmen from Southern states came on campus.

One time in the dining hall, Carver pulled up a chair at a table where a Southerner chewed away on his lunch. The student paused, then began fidgeting in his chair and rattling his silverware. Finally, the freshman stood up and moved to another table. As soon as the boy sat down, everyone at that table began rattling their silverware, got up, and sat with Carver.

As assistant botanist, Carver helped Louis Pammel with his research in mycology, the study of fungus. Carver added 1,500 specimens to the school's collection. Pammel was thrilled and said that he "was the most wonderful collector I ever have known." Carver's early morning walks almost always turned up some new mushroom or mold. He had been sharpening his botanist's eye his whole life, and now he was being recognized for it.

Carver worked on his final paper, "Plants as Modified by Man." In it he explained how a

Booker T. Washington.
Tuskegee University Archives, Tuskegee University

horticulturist could change the color or size or shape of a flower. "As the Chemist takes original elements or compounds, breaks up their combination or combines them into various proportions to fit his purpose, so we are to do the same without violating the laws of nature in the least." Carver saw man as "simply nature's agent or employee to assist her in her work." Before he finished his graduate studies, Alcorn College in Mississippi offered him a teaching position.

Carver's faculty friends at Iowa wrote glowing recommendations but did not want him to go. Professor Budd said he'd match any offer Alcorn

Booker T. Washington (1856–1915)

Much of Booker Taliaferro Washington's early life mirrored Carver's childhood. Washington was born into slavery, the son of a white father who owned Washington's mother. When the Civil War ended, Washington was nine years old. Like Carver, Washington struggled to get an education. Eventually, he became a student at Hampton Institute in Hampton, Virginia, where he militantly learned useful skills and was encouraged to teach others.

In 1881 Washington was hired to teach at the Tuskegee Normal and Industrial Institute, which sounded fancy, but was only 30 students in a rural clapboard church. He patterned the school after his education at Hampton, and worked tirelessly building the school and promoting his belief that African Americans could earn equality through hard work and education. He was a dynamic speaker and writer who gained the trust of white business leaders, and advised presidents on race relations and education.

Washington was married three times, and he had one daughter and two sons. He died in 1915 at the age of 59.

put out. And James Wilson said that IAC would find it "difficult, in fact impossible, to fill his place." Carver was flattered by the attention and the accolades, but while he was still considering the job, another offer came across his desk.

Carver opened the letter to read that Booker T. Washington, the principal of Tuskegee Institute, an all-black school in Alabama, wanted him to establish their agricultural department. Carver had heard about the institute. Washington believed that education was the path to equality. Tuskegee prided itself on its all-black faculty, which taught useful skills that would bring African Americans out of poverty as quickly as possible. In the letter, Washington offered Carver a teaching position.

Every African American knew about Washington. Just a year earlier, Washington delivered a much-publicized speech to the Cotton States and International Exposition in Atlanta, Georgia. In many ways, Carver agreed with what Washington had said in that speech and even embodied it. Washington said that all African Americans could succeed "by the productions of our hands." He suggested that instead of demanding equality, black people should work hard within white society to raise themselves up out of poverty.

Carver had done just that. He had worked hard for his education. In each town he passed through he had set up his own laundry business in order to pay his way. He never took charity, or fought for acceptance. He had earned his degree and his place in society. Carver also agreed with Washington that he should help his fellow African Americans.

Carver wavered for a week. He wanted to finish his master's degree in Iowa, and he was probably reluctant to, yet again, leave friends and a career he enjoyed. If he stayed in Iowa, Carver most likely would have become one of the premiere botanists of his time, or perhaps followed in the line of several of his professors and become secretary of agriculture. But the thrill of working with one of the great African American thinkers in a community that needed him desperately was an offer he could not refuse. "It has always been the one great ideal of my life," he said, "to be of the greatest good to the greatest number of 'my people' possible, and it is to this end I have been preparing myself for these many years; feeling as I do that this line of education is the key to unlock the golden door of freedom to our people."

Washington wrote back that the agricultural school would be "the best equipped and only distinct agricultural school in the South for the benefit of colored people." And offered him $1,000 a year in salary. Carver had had better offers, but Tuskegee with Washington at its head promised him the type of opportunity to serve that he was looking for.

Carver wrote back asking for space large enough to keep his prized botanical and rock collections: "I will accept the offer."

Over the summer of 1896, Carver hurriedly completed his graduate courses, and on Monday, October 5, he said good-bye to Iowa. His colleagues in the agricultural department presented him with a going-away gift: a gleaming new state-of-the-art microscope. With this gift under his arm, Carver left Iowa believing that he had finally found his calling. He would bring scientific agriculture to the poor African American farmers of the South. He would be part of Booker's mission to teach black people useful skills so they could gain equality by climbing the ladder of economic success. In the baggage compartment Carver had trunkloads of material to share, and his brain buzzed with all the information he could impart. But as the train headed south, its metallic rhythm began to pound doubts into his head.

Tuskegee seal. *Photo by author*

The Great Compromise

On September 18, 1895, Booker T. Washington spoke before a white audience of cotton growers and businessmen and assured them that the African American would be better off to "cast down your bucket where you are," which meant he should learn to live and work within the white community rather than fight to change it. Although Washington also told the white audience to cast down their buckets and work with the African American community, this speech became known as "the great compromise" because it seemed to accept segregation and discrimination. Washington did not speak of equality *now*, but believed that equality would arrive someday if black people educated themselves, developed marketable skills, and became successful economically. If you read the speech in its entirety, you will sense that he was walking a tightrope. He wanted to lift up African Americans, but he could not afford to annoy the white philanthropists who funded Tuskegee.

TUSKEGEE

Is the problem too difficult? No, all one needs is 25% patience and 75% of perseverance. —George Washington Carver

"When my train left the golden wheat fields and the tall green corn of Iowa for the acres of cotton, nothing but cotton, my heart sank a little," Carver said. He knew that moving to the Deep South meant that he'd encounter a different climate and different plants, but he was not prepared for the stark reality of the region as it rushed past his window in the "colored only" compartment of the train. "The scraggly cotton grew close to the cabin doors, a few lonesome collards, the only sign of vegetables; stunted cattle, bony mules; fields and hill sides cracked and scarred with gullies and deep ruts." All this devastation was the result of 100 years of cotton farming.

Before the Civil War, large plantations fueled by slave labor bundled and shipped acre upon acre of cotton to textile mills in the Northeast and Europe. The Civil War brought an end to slavery, but African Americans were still tied to cotton farming as tenant farmers or sharecroppers. With no means to support themselves, newly freed African Americans were forced into a system where a family worked a section of land in return for a share of the crops. The split was rarely fifty-fifty.

King Cotton

Since the invention of the cotton gin by Eli Whitney in 1793, cotton had become the main crop of the South. Before that, it took too much time and effort to pick the many seeds out of a cotton boll, the fluffy white "flower" of the cotton plant. The Whitney gin teased the seeds out in record time, making crops much more profitable. The more cotton a plantation grew, the more slaves it needed for harvest, creating a never-ending cycle of cotton exports and slave imports. By 1860 the South grew more than 75 percent of the world's cotton, and there were more than 3.5 million men, women, and children in bondage. When the Southern states broke away from the North, they mistakenly believed that "King Cotton" would allow them to win their independence.

Even though the South lost the war, and millions of people formerly enslaved were freed, the "cotton culture" continued. Planting the same crop in the same field year after year sucked vital nutrients from the soil, and after harvest, instead of plowing the cotton stalks under, it was easier to burn them to the ground, leaving the soil nearly lifeless. This process not only damaged the land but also harmed the farmers. As Carver noted when he arrived, "Everything looked hungry; the land, the cotton, the cattle, and the people."

The first cotton gin.
Courtesy of the Library of Congress, LC-USZ62-103801

Typically, a farmer was allowed to keep only a third of the crop. The rest was given to the white landowner. The farmers had to plant what the landowners wanted, and what they wanted was cotton. To make ends meet, sharecroppers planted as much as they could, often surrounding their entire cabin right up to the door with the crop.

Seeing the landscape, Carver must have realized he had found his mission in life. He would teach black farmers how to nourish the soil, grow better crops, and improve their lot in life. His mind was already full of agricultural techniques and ideas that he had learned from his professors. As Carver stepped off the train that idled on the edge of the small town of Tuskegee, where the clock tower of the redbrick Macon County courthouse loomed over the square, he was stepping into a different world. The only folks around were white. He would soon learn that African Americans only went to town on Saturdays to go to market. With his few personal possessions and his many academic specimens loaded into a wagon, he headed toward the school buoyed by a sense of purpose. Little did he know how soon he'd get that old sinking feeling in his heart again.

The New Kid

Back in Iowa, Carver was unique, and he was often treated with respect. Perhaps he thought he'd be treated just as kindly at Tuskegee, or that for the first time in a long time he'd be living among other African Americans and feel instantly at home. What he forgot was that he was the new

kid at school again, an outsider. He was from the North. He was educated in a white school and he did not have the same background as most of the teachers who were educated in all-black colleges.

Walking across the campus, the female teachers scowled at his now-three-year-old suit that Professor Pammel had bought him, his scuffed and dusty shoes, and his hand-sewn shirts. He looked more like a traveling salesman than a professor. Some teachers even judged him on his skin tone. In such a racially divided time, color mattered even among African Americans. Lighter skinned individuals tended to look down on those with

Sharecroppers pick cotton as the overseer rides by on horseback.
Courtesy of the Library of Congress, LC-USZ62-12511.

65

Gin Cotton

Ever wonder why Eli Whitney's cotton gin (short for engine) was so important? Find out with this simple activity. You will need whole raw cotton bolls that are available for purchase online. Look for natural bolls that have not been processed or cleaned.

Your goal is to pick out every seed stuck inside the cotton fiber. There may be as many as 40 seeds in one boll. Before you begin, make a space for three piles: the raw cotton bolls; the seeds (free of all fiber); and the "clean" fiber or lint (free of seeds and other debris). Set a timer to see how fast you can clean just one boll.

Before the cotton gin, adult slaves worked in the fields picking cotton, and then at night they worked by candlelight along with children and the elderly to clean the cotton. It took the average cotton picker an entire day to pick the seeds out of one pound of cotton (about 120 bolls). Multiply your time by 120 to find out how long it would take you to clean an entire pound. The first cotton gins made the process 50 times faster.

Cotton boll. *Photo by author*

darker skin, and Carver was darker than most of his fellow professors.

One day as he was chatting with Principal Washington, three teachers approached and asked Carver to identify some plants they had collected. Carver took the first wilted stalk and without hesitation pronounced the Latin scientific name, *Asarum canadense*, as well as the plant's common name, wild ginger. The second teacher handed him a plant: evening primrose, *Oenothera biennis*. As Carver identified each flower, the third professor flipped through a textbook to see if the cocky stranger from the North was correct. Carver knew they were trying to trick him and prove he was a fraud in front of Washington. Carver aced the test with his usual calm demeanor and tactfully avoided the three teachers after that.

It didn't help that Carver acted like he deserved special treatment. He was used to the standards at Iowa, and he expected to work in the same well-equipped environment that he'd left behind. Even before he stepped off the train in Tuskegee, Carver had asked Washington for rooms to house his botanical collection. These requests not only fell on deaf ears and weren't fulfilled, but they irked the other faculty members who thought his requests were arrogant. Carver was worried about mice and mold ruining his specimens and about not being able to access his books. The other teachers just thought, how dare he ask for two rooms when they had to share a room? In their opinion he acted as if he were a gift from God, rather than God's humble servant.

Plessy v. Ferguson

The year Carver arrived in Tuskegee, 1896, the US Supreme Court ruled on a case involving Homer Plessy, who refused to sit in a "colored only" train compartment. Plessy said that it violated his constitutional rights as an American citizen. The Court disagreed. This opened the door for more and more laws to create "separate but equal" facilities and services for people with darker skin. The lives of black people and white people became more and more separated, and a long way from equal. White lawmakers prevented African Americans from voting, getting a good education, and choosing a place to live. "Colored only" facilities were rarely in good repair and often were inconvenient. Public bathrooms might be located in a dank basement or even in another building. The federal law supporting "separate but equal" lasted until 1954.

Colored-only waiting room at a bus station. *Courtesy of the Library of Congress, LC-USF33-20522-M2*

(above) **The Milbank Agricultural Building.** *Photo by author*

(right) **Carver with an armload of new plant specimens.** *Tuskegee University Archives, Tuskegee University*

Trouble at Tuskegee

Carver expected a lot from Tuskegee, and the school expected a lot from him. He was director of the agriculture department, which in 1896 had only 13 students. But he soon had a two-page list of other responsibilities including managing two farms, the orchard, the beehives, and the dairy barn. He was expected to be the veterinarian for the farm animals, master gardener for the school grounds, and head of the unsanitary "sanitary closets" (toilets) that the school doctor warned could spread disease if not managed properly.

One day Carver recorded all of his activities. He started at 4:00 AM with his usual walk to refresh his soul and commune with nature. Students and townspeople got used to seeing him poking through hedgerows or digging at the side of the road at dawn if he spied a new specimen for his collection.

Carver ate breakfast with students in the dining hall, and then donned his teaching hat. "8:00 to 9:00 agri. Chemistry; 9:20 to 10:00, the foundation and harmony of color to the painter; 10:00 to 11:00, class for farmers," he wrote. In the afternoon he checked in on seven other classes, tested seeds, analyzed fertilizer, checked the poultry yard, and personally inspected 104 cows. That evening, as he did every evening, Carver answered letters and responded to the endless memos from Principal Washington.

Carver tackled every task thrown at him, but not without complaining. "I came knowing that I would encounter more difficulties in the way of proper sympathy and support," he wrote to Washington. "I knew it would not be an easy life to live. I am not seeking that just now, neither am I seeking personal aggrandizement. I only want to give the school my best service." In Carver's mind, his "best service" was developing, through thorough research, better farming practices for the county's poor black farmer. Principal Washington just wanted Carver to teach farming and manage the farms that produced all the food for the institute.

It wasn't just the enormous amount of work he had to do that bothered Carver, but Washington's style of micromanaging. Tuskegee was Washington's baby and nothing happened on campus without his approval. Carver, however, believed that as head of the agricultural department he should make decisions about the animals and crops. Washington would not let him. In 1898 Carver wrote a lengthy letter to the principal. "Now Mr. Washington, I think it ludicrously unfair to have persons sit in an office and dictate what I have to do and how I can do it," he wrote. "I simply want a chance to do what I know can be done." But that never happened while Washington was principal. He took his style of leadership from his mentor General Samuel Armstrong at Hampton College

in Virginia. And like the general, Washington even rode a horse around campus to inspect the grounds each day. If so much as a shovel was out of place, Carver was roused to put it away. Appearances mattered to Washington, who didn't want visitors to think the faculty and students were all "common country people."

It also bothered Carver that he was not given proper funding. Running a farm and creating an agricultural department cost money. Each time Carver asked for new equipment he was usually ignored or turned down. He understood and appreciated thriftiness; after all, he was the student who took notes on the back of book covers and

Building Tuskegee

Washington's school was a self-contained village of sorts. Students were taught useful skills like sewing, furniture making, and construction, by sewing all the students' clothes, crafting classroom desks and chairs, and hand-molding bricks to build the dormitories and classrooms. Every student also took turns working in the field, especially at harvest time. Everything grown on the farm was prepared by students and served at mealtime. If there was any surplus crop, it was sold in town.

Every brick used to build Tuskegee was made by hand by the students. *Photo by author*

(right) Much of Carver's early lab equipment was scrounged from the dump. *Tuskegee University Archives, Tuskegee University*

(below) Chemistry class. *Tuskegee University Archives, Tuskegee University*

ate weeds when his money ran out. But Washington had promised a well-equipped lab and Carver thought he should honor his promises. Carver had never let anyone stand in his way before, and he certainly would not let Washington undermine him.

When his chemistry students needed lab equipment that Washington declined to purchase, Carver marched the class out to the school dump. Knee-deep in busted chairs and smashed glass, he encouraged his students to see an object with fresh eyes. Don't look at what it was, he told them. See what it can be. In this way they turned broken bottles into funnels. Cracked and battered lanterns transformed into Bunsen burners.

Ox Bones and Humbugs

Carver never took classes on how to teach—it just came to him naturally. He was patient and methodical. Many of his students had little knowledge about plants or farming other than the physical work of planting or harvesting their family's crop. In class, Carver spoke in simple terms and often avoided technical jargon. He brought in armfuls of plants the students could hold and study, and he even wrote his own textbook called *Botany Made Easy*.

Carver was not the typical teacher. He didn't dress like a teacher, preferring comfort over style in his broken-in shoes and baggy trousers. New students often asked, "Who is that funny looking man?" He didn't lecture in the usual way either. Carver believed in sparking his students' curiosity

and allowing them to explore the subject at hand. He encouraged them to think for themselves in and out of class.

"This old notion of swallowing down other people's ideas and problems just as they've worked them out, without putting our brain and originality into it . . . must go."
—George Washington Carver

Carver also believed that "a large part of a child's education must be gotten outside of the four walls designated as classroom." So he was frequently traipsing off into the woods or cultivated fields with a flock of students behind him like dutiful ducklings. Whether they were artists like Carver or not, they all practiced drawing what they observed. It made the student take notice of tiny details that might make the difference between identifying one type of grass from another. They marveled at his skill and loved to test his abilities. One day, the entomology class presented him with an insect they had just "found." Carver studied the bizarre creature with its body of a beetle, head of an ant, and legs of a spider. Trying hard to keep a straight face, he declared it "a humbug."

(left) Teaching a botany class. *Tuskegee University Archives, Tuskegee University*

(above) Teaching outdoors. Washington insisted that all the students dress up even while working on the farm. *Tuskegee University Archives, Tuskegee University*

Drawing improved a scientist's eye for detail.
Photo by author, courtesy of the Tuskegee University Archives, Tuskegee University

71

DRAW NATURE

Carver believed that happiness and knowledge will come to you when you take time to look, listen, and live with nature. This exercise will help you get closer to the life around you.

YOU'LL NEED

■ Pencil

■ Notebook

Find a safe, quiet spot outside to sit and observe nature. It is all around you even if you live in a city. What do you see? A tree, bush, clouds, birds? Look closer. There is grass, a leaf, a weed, a bug. Choose one living thing to observe and draw. (It's best to pick something that does not move too quickly.) For example, draw a beetle. Not just any beetle, but one specific beetle you find.

Fix your eye on your nature model. What general shape does it have? Is it a triangle, an oval, circle, or rectangle? Draw that shape. What other general shapes do you see? Perhaps its body is an oval and its head is a square. Notice where the legs are attached. Are they short? Long? How do they bend? What is the texture of the beetle? Is it shiny smooth? How could you show that shininess? Or perhaps it is rough. What other details do you notice? Does it have antennae? A mouth? Wings? Jot notes down about how your nature model moves, what its habitat is like, noises it makes, or odors it gives off.

Don't fret if your first drawing isn't perfect. It is what you observed. And that is the important thing. You now know more about that living thing than you did before.

Tomorrow, find another nature model to draw and learn from.

Carver's teaching style matched his spiritual philosophy that all things are connected, and that it was important to understand the relationships between plants, animals, and the environment. So, a botany class might include a bit of history, geography, chemistry, art, and even poetry. Over the years the number of courses grew. He added animal nutrition, meteorology (weather), and the study of bacteria. The vast amount of knowledge that a farmer needed to be successful was daunting, and Carver emphasized that farming "requires the highest intelligence."

At other colleges, the agricultural classes were typically for men, but at Tuskegee, women were encouraged to attend. In long dresses and smocks, they learned gardening, poultry-raising, fruit cultivation, dairying, and beekeeping.

Carver was a rigorous teacher, but the students loved him. Yes, he had a funny voice, but students got used to that quickly. It was his kindness and excitement for his subject that drew students to him. He always had "time to say a kind word to a fellow or give him some good advice or food for thought," said one student. "How nice it would be if more of the teachers and instructors were that way."

Even students who weren't in Carver's classes sought him out. One female pupil remembered, "You'd always try to get up close enough for him to say something." One time she met him walking down Pearl Street. Just before he got to her, he reached down and picked up something. Curious, she asked, "Dr. Carver, what on earth could you find on this street?"

In the palm of his hand was a small white flower. "A wild strawberry blossom," he said. "See, you look, but you don't see."

More than anything, that is what Carver wanted his students to learn—to observe the beauty around them and enjoy the great web of organisms waiting to be understood. That was a common theme in his agricultural classes, his evening Bible study, and in later years his nature study for children. It took time, but even Washington finally admitted that Carver was "a great teacher, a great lecturer, a great inspirer of young men [and women]."

The Experiment Station

In February 1897, just four months after Carver arrived at Tuskegee, another job was piled on his already-filled plate. Tuskegee was chosen by the state as the site for a new agricultural experiment station, a regional research center for testing various farming methods, crops, fertilizers, and pest control. You'd think that with such a heavy workload, Carver would have objected. But he was delighted. This was his chance to do the kind of research that would most benefit those around him.

Carver's experiment station would be different from those in other states. Scientific agriculture meant the use of the latest technology and commercial fertilizer to increase production. But new technologies like tractors were expensive and beyond the reach of most Southern farmers who were locked in a system of sharecropping and debt. To make his experiment station most

Anatomy students learn about the ox from a skeleton of Betsy, one of the oxen that worked the school farm.
Tuskegee University Archives, Tuskegee University

Nature Study

In later years Carver taught nature study to teachers because, he said, "There is nothing better to interest the young mind than nature." It also got them on the path to learning more about agriculture. For the youngest child he encouraged exploration and making mud pies. Older students grew flowers in pots and tended a vegetable garden. One of Carver's nature study exercises instructed students to find a flea and observe how it moved. Imagine what your mother would say!

PLANT A WINDOW BOX

"There is nothing that adds so much of real beauty, cheerfulness, and instructive inspiration, for the small outlay as a few pots or boxes of well grown plants." —George Washington Carver

YOU'LL NEED

- Window box
- Potting soil
- Seeds or plants (Carver recommended growing herbs that are beautiful as well as useful—try parsley, thyme, basil, mint, or oregano)
- Notebook

1. Scoop the potting soil into the window box. Tamp down lightly. The top of the soil should be an inch below the rim of the box.

2. Plant the seeds or plants according to the package directions. Water, and place in a sunny window. Observe which seeds sprout first. Record their growth in a notebook. If you plant herbs like basil or thyme, try seasoning your food with a sprinkling of freshly chopped leaves.

effective, Carver insisted that all work be accomplished with the basic tools available to the local sharecropper: a hoe, a shovel, and maybe a plow drawn by a mule. "The Tuskegee station," he boasted, "has kept in mind the poor tenant farmer with one-horse equipment; so therefore, every operation performed has been within his reach."

Carver set up the experiment station initially on 10 acres of land that "had but little to characterize it other than its extreme poorness." It was badly eroded sandy soil that had been abused by cotton farming for decades. Carver knew it would be the perfect showcase for proper farming methods. Job number one was building up the soil.

Building the Soil

It was not a coincidence that black farmers worked the poorest soil. Although there was a black belt of rich dark soil running through Macon County, that land was owned by white farmers. African Americans struggled to coax seeds out of sandy soil riddled with gravel that didn't hold water and was easily washed away. "A poor soil produces only a poor people," Carver said. "Poor economically, poor spiritually and intellectually, poor physically." He believed that taking care of the soil was a moral responsibility.

Carver's Iowa teaching told him to use commercial fertilizer, which was specially blended with just the right amounts of key nutrients like nitrogen, phosphorus, and potassium. It was even endorsed by the US Department of Agriculture (USDA). But Carver had visited too many broken-down dusty shacks to know that most black share-croppers couldn't afford it. Animal manure spread on a field worked wonders, but many farmers in Macon County didn't even own their own mule. At plowing time they used the landowner's animal.

The answer to the farmers' soil problem was right beneath their feet. Every morning Carver was reminded of this as he walked along paths carpeted with pine needles or dried leaves.

Carver inspecting the experiment station. *Tuskegee University Archives, Tuskegee University*

Learning to plow with mules. *Tuskegee University Archives, Tuskegee University*

Carver instructed his students to fill in the eroded gullies with shovels full of "pine tops, hay, bark, old cotton stalks, leaves, etc. in fact, rubbish of any kind that would decay and ultimately make soil." An occasional load of earth was tossed on top. It might have been a hard sell because collecting organic material took a lot of time and effort, but Carver hoped that even the most overworked farmer would see how important it was, and that it was free.

The NPK of Feeding Plants

Every plant needs three basic key nutrients: nitrogen (N), phosphorus (P), and potassium (K).

Nitrogen promotes green leafy growth. Phosphorus nourishes the roots, flowers, and fruit, and potassium builds healthy stems. These nutrients are found in the soil and can be added with commercial fertilizer or compost. Some plants, like clover, beans, and peas, have their own system for getting nitrogen from the soil.

Carver also started a compost pile on campus where students dumped discarded paper, pulled weeds, tree trimmings, grass, and vegetable scraps from the school's kitchen. Occasionally he tossed swamp muck or rich loam from the forest floor onto the pile too. When the compost decayed into a rich dark brown and smelled of the earth, Carver spread it on the fields.

Eat the Weeds

Compost takes time to decay and add its nutrients to the soil. The farmers that George met on his daily ventures looked as if they needed proper nutrition right away. Again, he turned to Mother Nature.

Carver had been eating weeds since he was a boy picking ripe persimmons on the Carver farm. He ate dandelion greens, wild onions, plums, and milkweed pods. And from Aunt Mariah he learned plants' medicinal uses. In the experiment station's first easy-to-read informational bulletin, Carver encouraged farmers to collect acorns. They could

Build a Compost Bin

ADULT SUPERVISION REQUIRED

YOU'LL NEED

- Gloves
- Safety glasses
- Wire garden fencing (36 inches tall)
- Adult helper
- Measuring tape
- Wire cutters

1. Wearing gloves and safety glasses, unroll wire fencing with an adult's help. Hold in place and measure out 42 inches. Cut the fencing leaving wire ends long enough to fasten to the other side in step 2.

2. Bring the two ends together to form a cylinder. Bend the cut ends around the uncut edge to secure your bin. Stand your compost bin up and place it in a spot where it will not be disturbed.

3. Fill your bin. A healthy compost bin needs a balance of green compost (rich in nitrogen) and brown compost (rich in carbon). Green compost includes veggie scraps from the kitchen, grass clippings, pulled weeds, coffee grounds, fruit peels, and pulp. Brown compost includes dried leaves, newspaper, shredded mail, cardboard egg cartons, and other paper. For best results, rip items into small pieces before adding to the bin.

4. Keep your compost moist but not soggy. If it doesn't rain, sprinkle with water.

5. Occasionally stir the contents of the bin.

   Notice how the compost changes over time. The cantaloupe rind and egg carton will disappear as living microbes munch away, turning your garbage into food for your garden.

Cook with Weeds

"A good plate of dandelion greens," Carver said, made *"a dinner quite inexpensive but very appetizing."*

ADULT SUPERVISION REQUIRED

YOU'LL NEED

- Dandelion greens (two or three handfuls)
- Small saucepan
- 1 tablespoon butter
- Wooden spoon
- Salt and pepper

You will never go hungry if you learn to look for edible weeds. The most common is the dandelion. The green leaves are similar to spinach or kale, and best when picked in the spring before the yellow flower head appears. **Do not pick near roads, and avoid areas that have been sprayed with pesticides or herbicides.**

1. Wash the leaves and pat dry.

2. In a saucepan, melt a tablespoon of butter over low heat. Add the dandelion greens. Stir lightly with a wooden spoon for 2 to 3 minutes as they wilt and sauté in the butter.

3. Add pepper and salt to taste. Try the greens with a fried egg. That's how Carver liked them.

be fed whole to hogs or ground into flour as the Native Americans did and made into bread.

Cow Peas and Sweet Potatoes

Although cotton was the "scourge of the South," Principal Washington wanted Carver to continue growing and studying it. Carver skillfully created a cotton hybrid that increased the amount harvested by 200 percent. But he also experimented with other crops. He tested soil-building legumes like cowpeas, clover, and soybeans that could be plowed under as "green manure." Harvested, the cowpea made an excellent feed for livestock, and could be eaten in soups, stews, and Boston baked beans.

As early as 1903, Carver experimented with the peanut, but the sweet potato held his attention for several years. He tested the nutritional value of the sweet potato as well as the best way to grow it. The study of nutrition was relatively new at the turn of the century. Most people didn't know what a carbohydrate or a protein was, and it wasn't until 1912 that the word vitamin was used. People knew certain foods were good for them, but didn't know why. Carver was on the cutting edge of testing plants for their beneficial ingredients. For example, he determined that sweet potatoes contained 1.5 percent protein and 26.4 percent carbohydrates, but the vines, which people threw away, had 12.48 percent protein. Carver suggested feeding the vines to livestock to build muscle.

Although most of Carver's research notes have since been lost in a fire, we can still read the results because he published dozens of easy-to-read bulletins, which are packed with tables and charts showing the conditions and results of each test. He published more bulletins on the sweet potato than any other crop—six, compared to only two devoted to the peanut.

A Growing Partnership

"A soil's deficiency in nitrogen can be made up almost wholly by . . . keeping the legumes, or pod-bearing plants, growing upon the soil as much as possible." —George Washington Carver

Nitrogen, which is in the air around us, is necessary for every living thing. It gets into the soil when dead animals decompose. Plants take it up through their roots. But sometimes there is not enough of it. Legumes like peas and beans have a handy way of getting the nitrogen they need. It involves a partnership with the *Rhizobium* bacteria that attach to the roots of the plant. The bacteria take nitrogen from the air and "fix" it into a form the plant can use.

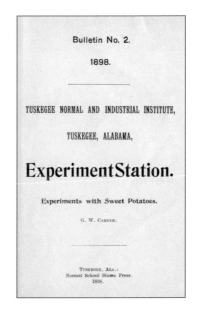

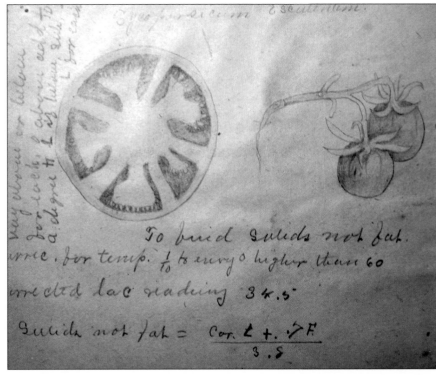

(top left) **Notes on the dandelion.** *Photo by author, courtesy of the Tuskegee University Archives, Tuskegee University*

(top right) **Bulletin No. 2, "Experiments with Sweet Potatoes."** *Tuskegee University Archives, Tuskegee University*

(left) **A page from one of Carver's research notebooks showing an ongoing study of the tomato.** *Photo by author, courtesy of the Tuskegee University Archives, Tuskegee University*

Grow Your Own Sweet Potato

"As a food for human consumption, the sweet potato has, and always will be held in very high esteem, and its popularity will increase as we learn more about its many possibilities." —George Washington Carver

The sweet potato was one of the first crops that Carver studied fully. He came up with more than 100 uses for the orange spud, and dozens of recipes.

The sweet potato (scientific name Ipomoea batatas) isn't really a potato. It is related to the morning glory, and you can see the resemblance in the leaves and flower of the plant. Originally found in South America, Christopher Columbus brought the sweet potato to Europe after landing in the West Indies.

YOU'LL NEED

- 1 sweet potato (fresh and firm)
- 4 toothpicks
- 1 glass jar
- Water

1. Using four toothpicks, suspend the sweet potato on the rim of the glass jar. Make sure the pointy end is on the bottom and under water. Place in a sunny spot and change the water once a week.

2. In a few days roots will form. Later, leaves and stems will sprout from the top. Continue to grow the plant in water. In a month or two, pot your new sweet potato plant in potting soil or in the garden. Observe how the plant grows in long trailing vines. In the fall, when growing season is over, pull up the roots to find more sweet potatoes.

Sweet potatoes.
Photo by author

> **"The primary idea in all of my work was to help the farmer and fill the poor man's dinner pail."**
> **—George Washington Carver**

Carver also added recipes to his bulletins. "It is just as important for the housewife," he said, "to use farm products wholesomely and economically as it is to produce them." Some of the recipes he reprinted from other sources, but many were his own concoctions. To test them he enlisted the help of Mrs. Wolcott and her two daughters.

Mrs. Wolcott taught English at the college and was one of the few on the faculty who was intrigued with Professor Carver's unusual ideas. He would stop by with a plate of greens or a sweet potato casserole and wait while the girls tasted it. Occasionally the dish was delicious and they told him so. But sometimes it was not. Instead of confessing the girls' dislike to the professor, Mrs. Wolcott would simply suggest he add a bit more of this or use less of that. She did not want to insult her colleague.

New Products

One day, Carver received a letter from a woman who had been growing peanuts for a number of years. But she didn't know what to do with them. Carver realized it was one thing to encourage farmers to grow new crops, but he had to also

Locally Grown

One day a local farmer invited Carver to dinner. As they sat down, Carver sighed with dismay at the food on the table. "Coffee from Brazil, macaroni from Italy, cheese from Wisconsin, bacon from Kansas." For dessert, they ate cake that was made from eggs purchased at a store and flour packaged in Minnesota. Carver appreciated the meal, but it must have cost the poor man a fortune. Here the man was growing inedible cotton instead of food he could eat and sell at market. How could Carver convince people like his host that they could eat better and save money if they raised their own food?

Many tenant farmers had no choice but to grow what the landowner wanted, which was usually cotton, so Carver encouraged farmers to add a vegetable garden and raise livestock alongside the cotton crops.

encourage a new market for that crop. Every plant has potential, Carver said. Its many uses lay hidden inside and it just took someone curious enough and skillful enough to unveil them.

In his laboratory, Carver ground up bits of hull and nut. He cooked them down and mixed them with different chemicals. Peanuts were high in oil, which he made into face lotion, soap, and axle grease. He used other parts of the plant for dyes, paper, rubber, linoleum. The peanut had limitless possibilities. All plants did, and the rest of Carver's life, he ground, swirled, mixed, and whirled, and created hundreds of products from dozens of plants.

Carver devised dozens of products using all parts of the peanut plant. *Photo by author*

(above) **Carver working in his lab.** *Tuskegee University Archives, Tuskegee University*

(right) **Carver was a big draw for farmers' picnics.** *Tuskegee University Archives, Tuskegee University*

GET READY
FOR THE
Farmers' Picnic
WHICH WILL BE HELD AT
Mt. Pleasant Church, One Mile South of Mathews,
Saturday, July 15th, 1905.

A GRAND SUBJECT FOR DEBATE.
"IS IT OUR DUTY TO EDUCATE OUR CHILDREN?"
This subject will be discussed by some of our ablest people, among whom are, Prof. John A. Wilson, of Montgomery, Ala.; Rev. Shepherd Scott, of Mamie, Ala.; Prof. Augustus Elmore, of Mathews, Ala.; Prof. Geo. W. Carver, of Tuskegee, Ala.; Mr. William Hinson, of Cecil, Ala.

ALL ARE INVITED TO ATTEND.
Prof. Geo. W. Carver is one of the best educated men in our colored race. If your soil don't produce crops well bring some with you and he will tell you the reason why. Some of your fruit trees are failing to bear as they should, break off a small branch and bring it with you, and you will be told the cause. Any question on any kind of plant or any kind of soil you are at liberty to ask him; he is the man to answer.
Don't miss this Grand Picnic. Come and be with us, and feast on the many delicacies we are going to have. Bring tables if desired. Flying Jennies, Watermelon Wagons, etc. Taxes on Tables 25c., Flying Jennies 88.00, Watermelon wagons 15c.

FRANK HINSON, President
ARTHUR BURKE, Secretary.

"The Man to Answer"

Researching new crops, processes, and products was only one part of the experiment station. The other part was getting that information out to the farmer. Several years before Carver arrived at Tuskegee, Washington held an annual Negro Farmers' Conference. Hundreds of farmers showed up to share their concerns and attend lectures. When Carver arrived, he expanded on the idea and taught monthly Farmers' Institutes where he shared practical advice and hands-on experience. He demonstrated how to raise chickens, how to prepare the land for cotton, and how to recognize and destroy destructive insects.

Advertisements posted all around the county boasted of George's abilities: "If your soil don't produce crops well bring some with you and he will tell you the reason why. Some of your fruit trees are failing to bear . . . break off a small branch and bring it with you. . . . Any questions on any kind of plant or any kind of soil you are at liberty to ask him; he is the man to answer."

Between his bulletins, conferences, and classes, Carver reached thousands of people, but there were many folks that could not or would not travel, and many others could not read his bulletins. To reach them, he "put a few tools and demonstration exhibits in a buggy and set out . . . on Saturday afternoons, to visit rural areas near Tuskegee." He loved to chat with folks. He met them after church and outside schools. Women crowded around Carver's "fancy work," his crochet and knitting. After convincing them that yes, he did make them, he demonstrated how to embroider on feed sacks to make chair covers or a tablecloth.

Carver's weekend demonstrations were a hit, but he could not do them full time. In 1906, Principal Washington found Morris K. Jesup, a banker from New York who donated money for the creation of a movable school. Carver sketched a design, and boys from the institute built the wagon. The first trip was launched in May with George Bridgeforth holding the reins.

It was such a success that the US Department of Agriculture adopted it. The USDA hired one of Carver's students, Thomas Campbell, to run the

The Jesup Wagon in action. *Tuskegee University Archives, Tuskegee University*

Thomas M. Campbell

Born in 1883, Thomas Campbell was one of Carver's most successful students. When Campbell first got to Tuskegee, he was asked if he wanted to be in the farming program. He answered, "No. I came to school to get away from the farm." Then he was asked to join the agriculture department. Not understanding the meaning of the word agriculture, he said, "Sure. That sounds like fun." But with Carver as his teacher, Campbell grew to love the science of agriculture. For extra credit he even put together a hog skeleton for display in the agriculture department.

When the USDA was looking for someone to drive the first movable school, Carver recommended Campbell. He was not only the first cooperative extension agent in the United States but also the first African American field agent in the USDA.

He wrote *The Movable School Goes to the Negro Farmer.* And in 1930, Campbell earned the Harmon Award for service to American agriculture and education. Campbell and his wife Anna had six children. Their fourth child, William, went to Tuskegee and became a highly decorated member of the Tuskegee Airmen, a group of African American WWII fighter pilots.

Bust of Thomas Campbell. *Photo by author*

83

program. In 1907, Campbell traveled more than 800 miles within the county. When most employees in the department were white, having a black agent was another Tuskegee accomplishment. However, since Tuskegee wasn't technically a land-grant college, the movable school was moved to Alabama Polytechnic Institute (now Auburn University), a white school. But Carver and Washington were proud that their Jesup Wagon became the model for future farm extension programs.

The Clay Beneath His Feet

Another one of Carver's many projects was the creation of paints from clay. Ever since he was a small boy on the Carver farm, he had been playing around with natural pigments, mashing red berries, or grinding brown nuts with a rock. He never lost his knack of spying a new color source. One day Carver was out inspecting a herd of cows when he happened to notice the clay beneath his feet. He dug up a fistful and carried it back to his lab.

Boiling the clay and straining it, Carver developed an inexpensive paint for local farmers. Macon County's soil ranged from snow white and pale cream, to brilliant yellow and fiery red, offering an endless number of combinations. By adding bluing to the white clay, Carver created a royal blue similar in color to the paint Egyptians used to decorate a pharaoh's tomb. Carver just hoped the paint would "aid the farmer in tidying up his premises both in and outside making his surroundings more healthful, more cheerful and more beautiful."

Carver took paint samples to fairs and conferences. Several paint companies expressed interest in his formulas, which he gladly gave. He wasn't particularly interested in selling them commercially. He was already pursuing another topic or getting ready to give another speech.

Carver holding a clod of earth.
Tuskegee University Archives, Tuskegee University

Long before television, lectures were a popular form of entertainment, and Carver was surprised and delighted to receive more invitations to speak. A newspaper could describe the 15 wood stains and 13 paints he had developed, but you had to see his royal blue in person to grasp the awe of such a glorious color hidden in a clump of clay. Carver spent weeks creating exhibits people could see and touch. And he provided clear instructions so folks could easily duplicate his methods.

While some people at the institute scoffed at Carver's projects, his ideas were gaining a wider audience. Only Principal Washington lectured off campus more than Carver did.

Carver inspects paint samples. *Tuskegee University Archives, Tuskegee University*

"Bent Upon Bloodshed"

George Washington Carver enjoyed traveling the countryside, but on one occasion he expressed serious doubt "as to whether I would return to Tuskegee alive or not as the people were thoroughly bent upon bloodshed." On a trip to Ramer, Alabama, Carver met Miss Frances Johnston, a photographer documenting African American schools. She was meeting teacher Nelson Henry, who Carver knew. As the train pulled into the station, Carver noticed a crowd. Thankfully, nothing happened as the young, white photographer rode off with the African American teacher.

Carver went on to the house where he was staying. A short time later he heard pounding on the door. It was Miss Johnston disheveled and scared. A gang of white men had stopped them on the road, furious to see a black man alone with a white woman. One thug shot at Henry three times, but Henry managed to leap out of the buggy and run.

Carver hurried Miss Johnston to the next train station knowing if they were caught he would be shot at too. Once she was safe, Carver walked back to Ramer keeping to the shadows and corn fields. As the sun rose the next morning Carver watched as a man armed with a shotgun patrolled in front of the schoolhouse. A posse of 12 had their horses saddled and ready to ride. Carver sent word to Mr. Henry "to flee for his life, which he did." But the gang was still looking for the black man who took Miss Johnston to the train station. When Carver reported the incident to Principal Washington he said it was "the most frightful experience of my life."

Statue of Booker T. Washington "lifting the veil of ignorance" from the figure of a slave.
Photo by author

5

PEANUT FAME

How far you go in life depends on your being tender with the young, compassionate with the aged, sympathetic with the striving, and tolerant of the weak and the strong. Because someday in life you will have been all of these. —George Washington Carver

On November 14, 1915, Booker T. Washington died. He and George Washington Carver had argued about almost everything except their joint mission to raise people up from poverty through education. Now Washington was gone and George could only remember the bad words said between them. "I am sure Mr. Washington never knew how much I loved him, and the cause for which he gave his life," he told a friend. It hurt to know that the person who gave him the opportunity of a lifetime was now gone.

Robert Russa Moton became the new principal of Tuskegee. He allowed Carver more freedom for research. Moton knew that with Washington gone, Carver was the most famous man on campus. He decreased Carver's teaching schedule and encouraged him to accept more speaking engagements.

Living Fire

For the most part Carver enjoyed being in the spotlight. Although he was normally shy unless with friends, he was able to use his skills developed as an actor on the college stage to captivate his audiences. However, the enthusiasm he brought to his subject matter wasn't an act. He loved talking about nature, farming, and developing new products. The chancellor of the University of Georgia heard Carver and said, "that was the best lecture on agriculture to which it has ever been my privilege to listen." Carver had a knack for explaining difficult scientific processes so that the average person could understand. A talent, said the chancellor, "which is possessed by only five or six men in the entire country."

Carver spoke as easily to a hundred people as he did to one person. He often had to give two speeches in one town; one to a black audience and one to a white audience. His message and tone never varied regardless of who packed the hall. He had a light musical voice and told stories to get his message across. "The most striking thing about him is his eyes," said one listener, "which are deep black but which seem to have two gleaming coals of living fire behind them."

The name George Washington Carver on a program guaranteed a packed house, and his schedules were exhausting. His itinerary on one Sunday started with a speech to an adult Sunday school group, followed by a discussion with children. After a hearty church supper, Carver was treated to a tour of the town, and then participated in a two-hour round table discussion. In the evening, he gave his main lecture, chatted with audience members, and then people followed him back to his room to pepper him with more questions. "So you see," he said. "I had a very, very busy day."

Robert Russa Moton (1867–1940)

Born in Virginia, Moton grew up and attended Hampton Institute as Washington had. After graduation he worked at Hampton until 1915, when he went to Tuskegee. In 1918, President Woodrow Wilson sent Moton to Europe to investigate racism against black soldiers during World War I, and later Moton helped establish a veteran's hospital at Tuskegee. Moton retired from the institute in 1935 and died five years later in 1940.

Robert Russa Moton.
Tuskegee University Archives,
Tuskegee University

One speaking engagement led to another, and like a stone tossed into a pond, the ripple of Carver's influence expanded from Macon County and the state of Alabama, throughout the South, to the rest of the country and the world. In 1916, he was asked to serve on the advisory board of the National Agricultural Society, and he became a fellow of Great Britain's Royal Society of Arts.

As he became more famous, he received more invitations from traditionally white organizations. Carver knew that each time he stepped on stage it advanced the cause for every African American, even though he rarely spoke directly about race relations. Accepting a speaking invitation meant rigorous planning—he couldn't just jump on a train and go. A black man traveling throughout the South had to scour the train schedule for a "colored only" car and check the route for hotels that would allow him to stay. A map of his itinerary looked like a hopscotch across the states just so he could be assured a place to sleep at night. Carver might have been famous, but he was still black, and even though white audiences clamored to hear him speak, he was still subjected to the same senseless racism.

When Carver arrived at the venue, he was usually directed to a back stairway, or brought in through a rear door. He couldn't even walk through the same entrance as the guests who had paid money to hear him speak. It didn't help matters that he often looked more like a "field hand than a professor," with his worn and baggy trousers, floppy cap, and threadbare coat. He was not what audiences expected. But Carver did not

Carver ready to travel. *Tuskegee University Archives, Tuskegee University*

believe in changing his style to suit someone else. He preferred to wear his comfortable, old clothes, even when the college encouraged him to purchase new ones. One time he even confessed, "I don't want to wear shoes, but I do it—to escape undesirable publicity."

Wheat for the World

World War I (WWI) officially began in 1914 when Great Britain, France, and their Allies battled Germany, Bulgaria, and Austria-Hungary, as well as the Ottoman Empire. But the United States did not enter the war until 1917. Because of the war, many American merchant ships had been sunk, preventing much-needed foreign supplies like rubber and dyes from entering the country. The federal government called for conservation and actively sought substitutes for these valuable commodities. Carver had already explored a rubber material from the sweet potato, and he felt his clay pigments worked just as well as those from Germany. Although both products had potential they were never manufactured for the war effort.

In January 1918, David Fairchild of the USDA asked Carver to come to Washington, DC, to talk about the wheat shortage. Much of the American crop had been sent oversees to feed a starving Europe and to fuel US soldiers. Carver had been conserving wheat at the institute by teaching the cooking staff how to make bread with a combination of wheat and sweet potato flours.

Carver met with Fairchild and the committee and then demonstrated how to make his bread. He was gratified to be treated like an equal among government officials. "Not one time," he said, "has colored been mentioned." Other food experts clamored for Carver's opinion on their products. At the end of the meeting, Fairchild banged his

World War I Poster. *Courtesy of Documenting the American South, UNC-Chapel Hill Library*

Food Will Win the War

On August 10, 1917, the USDA set up a wartime conservation effort headed by Herbert Hoover, who would later become the 31st US president. American farmers rushed to increase productivity by moving into the Great Plains and using more mechanized equipment. Hoover made it voluntary but patriotic to eat less meat, wheat, fats, and sugar. "Food will win the war," Hoover said. He promoted meatless Mondays and wheatless Wednesdays. Because of the widespread participation in the campaign, food shipments to Europe doubled within a year. It is estimated that America's relief efforts saved 350 million people during and after WWI.

fist on the table and said, "We must do something now." The USDA ordered an industrial food drier capable of processing 10,000 pounds of sweet potatoes to fuel more experiments similar to those Carver had conducted.

Richer Than We Think We Are

World War I didn't just prevent products from getting into the United States; it also blocked goods from getting out. Cotton exports fell drastically, crushing the already flat economy of the South. It became even more important to compost waste and reuse materials. When there was no money for household items, Carver showed people how to make rugs out of discarded cotton stalks. Strips of burlap, bits of rope, old rags, and bark from the poplar tree could be woven onto looms to make fabric. Bacon fat could be made into soap, and inedible watermelon rinds could be made delicious by pickling.

**"My work is that of conservation . . . the saving of things that the average person throws away."
—George Washington Carver**

"It is estimated that fully two-thirds of our fruits and half our vegetables go to waste every year," Carver said in bulletin #27. He instructed folks to preserve their produce by canning, pick-

The Search for American-Made Rubber

Carver was not the only one looking for a substitute for foreign rubber. Thomas Edison, Henry Ford, and Harvey Firestone teamed up in 1927 to create the Edison Botanical Research Corporation. They sent out hundreds of botanists to collect plants from all over the world and tested 17,000 species including Carver's sweet potato. Edison favored goldenrod because it contained 12 percent natural latex, the material needed to make rubber.

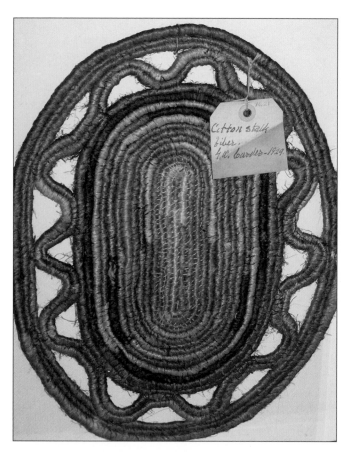

Rug woven from discarded cotton stalks. *Photo by author*

Pickle Watermelon Rinds

Carver believed that something only went to waste because we hadn't figured out a use for it yet. Well, here is a great use for something most people throw away—watermelon rinds. Turn them into delicious pickles.

ADULT SUPERVISION REQUIRED

YOU'LL NEED

- 4 cups peeled, cubed watermelon rind (the green and pink removed)
- ¾ cup sugar
- 1 cup vinegar
- 2 sticks of cinnamon
- 1 teaspoon whole cloves
- Large saucepan
- Spoon
- Airtight container

1. With a vegetable peeler, take off the hard dark-green skin to reveal the white part beneath. Trim off most of the pink flesh, too. Cut the white rind into one-inch cubes.

2. Add all the ingredients to a large saucepan. Bring to a boil, stirring occasionally. Reduce heat, cover, and simmer for 45 to 60 minutes or until the cubes turn translucent. Let cool.

   Refrigerate for 24 hours before serving.

3. Store in an airtight container in the refrigerator for up to 2 weeks.

---

ling, and drying. In a belt-tightening time his message was, "We are richer than we think we are."

The Peanut

Carver continued his work on the peanut, which had been growing in popularity among Southern farmers because the boll weevil had devastated cotton crops. Carver must have been gratified to see the vast white cotton fields replaced with acres of rich green peanut plants. He'd been pushing the peanut and other soil-building legumes for 20 years, but it took a ravenous pest to finally change farmers' minds.

In order to boost the market for the burgeoning crop, Carver developed dozens of products made from various parts of the peanut and published a bulletin with 105 recipes. Some dishes were more digestible than others. Peanut sausage was a steamed concoction of nuts and mashed bananas with the texture of beef and served with a tomato sauce.

On September 22, 1919, Carver mentioned to principal Moton that he had just created a tasty peanut milk by soaking peanuts in water, then grinding them and straining out the liquid. A week later he got a letter from Walter Grubbs of the newly formed Peanut Products Corporation in Birmingham, Alabama, asking for more details. Carver, in his most enthusiastic manner, wrote back, "I think I am conservative in my statement when I say that it is without a doubt, the most wonderful product that I have yet been able to work out, and I see within it, unlimited possibilities." Grubbs invited Carver to speak at the dedication of the boll weevil monument that was being erected in Enterprise, Alabama. Bad rainstorms prevented Carver from attending, but Grubb and other peanut farmers realized there was no better person to be a spokesperson for the peanut than George Washington Carver.

A year later, in 1920, the United Peanut Association of America invited Carver to speak at their conference in Montgomery, Alabama. Carver arrived at the hotel carrying two large black bags filled with peanut products and informed the man at the desk that he was speaking at the conference. Eyeing him suspiciously, the clerk directed him to the freight elevator. As the elevator cranked and clanked up to the convention hall, Carver readied himself and his props.

The audience of mostly white middle-aged peanut growers were not keen on this black man standing before them. What could *he* possibly tell *them* about peanuts? His soprano voice startled the audience to attention. But the more Carver spoke,

George Washington Carver working in lab. *Tuskegee University Archives, Tuskegee University*

Goobers and Groundnuts

Also known as the peanut, this plant is well named because it's a legume like the pea, and it's used like a nut. But it is a truly unique plant. Each summer small yellow flowers appear and self-pollinate. The ovary or seed develops in the center of the flower. When the petal falls off, the stem is called a peg. The peg bends down and burrows back into the earth where the fruit, which is the peanut, grows. The whole process from seed to harvest takes four to five months.

Today, the United States grows more than two and a half million tons of peanuts each year. *Photo by author*

Bake Peanut Strip Cookies with Bananas

This recipe is adapted from one of Carver's "105 Ways of Human Consumption" of the peanut. His recipes, like all recipes of that time period, tended to be vague and lacked important details like oven temperature or length of time to bake. But that is understandable because ovens in the early 1900s did not have temperature gauges or timers. Carver said to bake these cookies (number 36 in the list) in a "quick oven." Although Carver called these "peanut strip cookies," this recipe suggests making them as drop cookies for the best results

---

ADULT SUPERVISION REQUIRED

YOU'LL NEED

- Cookie sheet, greased
- Food processor (or blender)
- 1½ cups unsalted peanuts
- Mixing bowl
- 2 cups mashed banana (about 4 whole, peeled bananas)
- Fork
- 1½ cups oats (old fashioned or quick oats)
- 1½ cups flour
- 1 cup sugar
- ½ cup butter, softened (one stick)
- 1 teaspoon salt
- Spoon

1. Preheat oven to 350°F.
2. Grease a cookie sheet and set aside.
3. In a food processor grind 1½ cups unsalted peanuts until fine but not oily and set aside.
4. In a mixing bowl, mash bananas with a fork until nearly smooth. Add the other ingredients and stir with large spoon till well blended.
5. Drop by spoonful onto cookie sheet, about an inch apart. Bake for 15 minutes until underside is lightly browned.

Makes three dozen cookies.

the deeper they fell under his spell. As one newspaper put it, "Dr. Carver verily won his way into the hearts of the peanut men." The council voted to help Carver secure any patents that he might want to apply for, but Carver had no need for patents. He was more interested in getting his message out than mass-producing a product.

News of his peanut milk made it into the pages of *Good Health* magazine and *Popular Mechanics*. Today we have soy milk, almond milk, and rice milk, but in Carver's day, there was no other nondairy variety to help children with milk allergies. A missionary from the African Belgian Congo (now called Democratic Republic of the Congo) asked for the recipe. The nutritious nondairy milk was ideal for feeding starving children who lived in villages without cows or electricity for refrigeration.

Speaking Before the House

In 1921, the US House of Representatives Ways and Means Committee called Carver to testify on behalf of a peanut tariff. American peanut farmers wanted a tax on the importation of peanuts to protect them from too much competition from foreign growers.

Joseph W. Fordney, head of the tariff committee, sat in the center of the large semicircular desk. Other members of Congress sat on either side. The ends of the desk curved around one lone table in the center of the room. Behind that table stood Carver.

Wearing his famous Iowa suit rather than the outfit the peanut council gave him, Carver spent

The Boll Weevil

A small grey-brown beetle with the snout of an anteater is credited for ending the stranglehold cotton had on the Southern farmer. Originally found in Mexico, the weevil moved north, laying its eggs in, feeding on, and destroying cotton buds. Although many farmers had started to diversify their crops because of the terrible toll cotton placed on the soil, the infestation of the boll weevil sped up the process. In 1919, the town of Enterprise, Alabama, erected a statue to the boll weevil with this inscription: "In profound appreciation of the Boll Weevil and what it has done as the Herald of Prosperity."

Boll weevil statue in Enterprise, Alabama.
Courtesy of the Library of Congress,
LC-DIG-highsm-07155

the first few minutes of his 10-minute time slot taking jars and bundles from his bag. Someone cracked a joke, but Carver didn't pay attention to the snide comment or the laughter that followed.

The congressman from Texas quieted the room and assured the committee that what they were about to see was not a joke. "This man," he said, "knows a great deal about this business. Let us have order."

Just as he had done hundreds of other times, Carver held up a bottle like a magician brandishing a rabbit from his hat: a glass jar of peanut milk, a coffee substitute, candy, fabric dye. With each product he explained in the same terms he would use with a child visiting a farmer's fair how they were made. When his 10 minutes were up, the chairman waved his hand. "Your time is unlimited," he said. Carver continued: face lotion, livestock feed, axle grease. The politicians leaned over the railing as spellbound as if he were pulling a never-ending scarf from his sleeve.

At one point Carver held up a breakfast bar that he made from sweet potatoes and peanuts and said, "I am very sorry you cannot taste this, so I will taste it for you." The congressmen laughed as he took a bite.

When the representative from Connecticut made a racial comment, Carver calmly brought the conversation back to the matter at hand. Of the tariff, Carver said, "We could not allow other countries to come in and take our rights away from us."

"If American peanuts were superior to foreign ones, they shouldn't need protection," one representative suggested.

Carver simply said, "Sometimes you have to protect a good thing."

When Carver was through, the committee applauded. In less than an hour he had convinced them to support the tariff.

Most big city newspapers covered the hearing and forever after Carver was linked to the peanut. He became a household name, even in the home of Thomas Edison, who offered him a job in New Jersey. Carver declined, saying he wouldn't want to work on research that was not his own.

He felt the same way with business. He was happier advising others, as he did for the Ralston-Purina Company that was interested in his tasty breakfast bar, and paint companies interested in his paint formulas.

Who Invented Peanut Butter?

Although Carver developed more than 300 products from the peanut, he did not invent peanut butter. In South America, the ancient Inca civilization ground peanuts to make a paste. In the United States, John Harvey Kellogg, who became famous for his cereal, patented a method for making peanut butter in 1895. In 1903, Dr. Ambrose Straub patented a peanut butter machine. The first commercial peanut butter was introduced at the St. Louis World's Fair in 1904.

Carver and friends from Tuskegee did create the Carver Products Company, and he developed Penol, a medicine for respiratory ailments made from peanut oil and creosote. But Carver apparently preferred to be in the lab. He did eventually hold three patents, one for Penol and two for paints, but he was happiest when he was uncovering the mysteries hidden inside plants and breaking new ground.

A Year of Contradictions

In 1923, Carver received two honors that showed how vast his sphere of influence had become. The first came from the United Daughters of the Confederacy expressing appreciation for his work. There were few organizations with a more conservative background, and it contrasted sharply with the National Association for the Advancement of Colored People (NAACP). Founded in 1909 as an alternative to Booker T. Washington's accommodationist stance, the NAACP gave Carver the Spingarn Medal because his "clear thought and straightforward attitude have greatly increased inter-racial knowledge and respect." Carver probably saw the irony in the support he received from both groups, but he was optimistic that his work in some little way was bringing people together.

That same year a section of land where Carver liked to meander was being transformed into a much-needed veteran's hospital. More than 300,000 African American men had fought in the US Army's segregated units in WWI, but when these men came home they did not receive a hero's welcome. Instead they were refused care at many area hospitals. After much debate, the government began construction on a blacks-only facility at Tuskegee.

George and everyone else on campus were thrilled that the hospital would be staffed by African Americans. This was important because it was illegal for a white nurse to touch a black person. There always had to be an African American aide nearby to carry out a doctor's orders. Many prominent white Tuskegeeans, however, some of whom Carver considered friends, insisted that whites be in charge. Once again Carver's place on the tightrope of race relations wobbled. He must have wondered why his friendship hadn't altered his friends' views on the role African Americans could play in society.

When Moton pushed for the all-black staff, he received death threats, and when the first black employee arrived, so did the Ku Klux Klan. Friends urged Carver to leave, but he stayed put. Perhaps he watched out his window as 700 ghostly robed figures marched through town and past the campus entrance. The hooded figures did not say a word, but their heavy footsteps and eerie silence spoke volumes. President Warren G. Harding had to step in, and eventually Tuskegee was allowed to staff the hospital with African American doctors and nurses.

Reluctant Rights Activist

In 1925 Carver said, "I am away from the school so much that it is impossible to conduct a scientific

Penol was made with peanut oil and creosote. *Photo by author*

> **"Without genuine love for humanity it is impossible to accomplish much in this question of the races. . . . Each individual, no matter what his color or creed, has his particular task to do in life."**

experiment of value." He closed the experiment station so he could concentrate on spreading his message to a wider audience. His greatest impact may have been at traditionally all-white Southern schools like Clemson Agricultural College. To many on campus his presence was a "distinct shock" that hopefully jarred them out of their hateful racist thinking. The president of the college said, "There is no better way to create a proper relationship between the two races."

Carver's opinion on race was that there was no such thing. It was a wrongheaded false distinction created by fear and hate. There is "no question or questions peculiar to the Negro," he said. All social problems were "simply a problem of humanity." In this sense Carver was color-blind. Although he had felt the brutality of other people's racism, he tried to treat everyone the same. He believed in the Golden Rule: Do unto others as you would have them do unto you. Unlike Booker T. Washington who spoke directly to the issue, Carver served up his views on race not so much with words, but with his actions and his attitude. In speeches he couched his message in stories about nature. He'd hold up a lump of grey Alabama clay or a handful of tiny peanuts and talk about the untapped potential inside. Everyone in the audience knew what he was saying. Inside every person was untapped genius waiting to be discovered.

The Blue Ridge Boys

Carver worked closely with the Commission on Interracial Cooperation and the YMCA. As a college student, Carver had attended a YMCA summer school, and he was pleased to be going as a main speaker to the one in Blue Ridge, North Carolina. The first time he had attended such a camp he had to eat and room alone. Now, even as a well-known figure, the situation wasn't that different. However, there was a glimmer of hope. One student, Howard Kester from Lynchburg College in Virginia, invited Carver to stay in his cabin. But the dining hall remained closed to him.

As he ate a light meal alone in his room, Carver thought about the rumor he had heard that two boys were going to stand up and walk out on his speech in protest. He wondered if they would. It would not change his message, or prevent him from speaking, so it didn't matter.

That evening when Carver walked to the microphone a hush fell over the audience. Everyone was waiting for the protest. But not a soul budged. After the speech, Carver graciously greeted a long line of students eager to shake his hand. One boy looked more sheepish than all the others. He admitted that he was going to walk out, then he thrust out his hand and Carver shook it, accepting the boy's apology.

It was occasions like this that made his group of "Blue Ridge Boys" grow. Over the years, Carver had made many friends when he spoke on college campuses. Many were white, and some were grandsons of Southern slaveholders. But they all admired Carver, respected his message, and appreciated his friendship and guidance.

Some of his "boys," as he called them, went on to become activists. Howard Kester, for example, helped organize the Southern Tenant Farmers Union in 1934 to advocate for poor farmers of all races. But some of the students he motivated quickly discovered the hateful backlash for standing up for equality. One student in Texas complained when her college canceled Carver's lecture. She wrote an editorial in which she said, "You have shown me the one race, the human race. Color of skin, or form of hair mean nothing to me now, but length, and width, and bredth [sic] of soul and loving kindness mean everything." The college punished her for such liberal thinking by taking away her scholarship.

No Real Scientist

George Washington Carver had had a lifetime of practice turning the other cheek when called names or treated like dirt, but there was one criticism that he could not tolerate. On November 18, 1924, Carver, now 60 years old, was in New York City to speak to the Women's Board of Domestic Missions of the Reformed Church in America. His thin voice rose up into the soaring golden ceiling of the sanctuary. He held up bottles and jars that glistened in the light from so many chandeliers. "No books ever go into my laboratory," he said. "I never have to grope for methods; the method is revealed at the moment I am inspired to create something new." It was a speech he had given dozens of times before. His work, he said, was guided by the plants or rocks in front of him, God's creations. But the next morning he woke to find a biting editorial in the newspaper. The reporter condemned Carver's methods, saying, "Men of Science Never Talk that Way." The article went on to say, "Real chemists, or at any rate other real chemists, do not scorn books." They did not rely on "inspiration." The reporter hinted that Carver's unscientific talk reflected poorly on Tuskegee as well as all African Americans.

The criticism stung. Carver did not have any intention of leaving his audience with the idea that his work was unscientific. He responded to the editorial with one of his own. The *New York World* never printed it, but other newspapers did. In it Carver clarified what he meant by inspiration.

> "Inspiration is never at variance with information; in fact, the more information one has, the greater will be the inspiration."
> —George Washington Carver

This was similar to what the French scientist Louis Pasteur once said: chance favors a prepared mind. Pasteur went on to invent the process of pasteurizing milk.

As an example of Carver's inspiration, he mentioned several ideas that came to him as he wandered through a city market. Eyeing the taro and yautias, "dozens of things came to me. None of which could be found in a book." His thoughts of how to utilize vegetables that he had never seen before came to him because he had such a vast knowledge about similar produce. He ended his editorial with, "If this is not inspiration and information from a source greater than myself, kindly tell me what it is."

To Carver, faith and science were deeply connected. Today scientists still don't understand how a thought is made. Almost 100 years ago, Carver chose to believe in a higher source, rather than his own ability. He couldn't have sounded more like a scientist than when he said, "Science is simply the truth."

An editorial cartoon of the Pullman coach system. *From McCutcheon, The Mysterious Stranger and Other Cartoons, courtesy of Google Books*

Derailed at the Station

By 1930 Carver received so many invitations that Tuskegee hired a traveling secretary to make the arrangements. H. O. Abbott coordinated all of his trips, including a 15-day circuit through Kansas, Oklahoma, and Texas. Carver spoke to black audiences, white audiences, scientists, teachers, and Christian organizations. Abbott soon discovered what Carver already knew: that travel for a black man was tricky.

By phone, Abbott reserved two sleeping compartments on a Pullman car that would take them from Oklahoma City to Dallas, Texas. After a full day of speaking, shaking hands, and chitchat, Carver was exhausted and ready to climb into a sleeping berth and let the rhythm of the train rock him to sleep. But when they arrived at the station, the railroad agent refused to let them board. No amount of arguing would change the man's mind. No black men were sleeping on the Pullman car with white folks, and this train did not have a sleeping car for black people. Finally, Carver and Abbott lugged their suitcases down the long line of cars to the end where they sat up all night in the "colored only" compartment.

News of the incident spread quickly, and the next morning the Oklahoma City *Black Dispatch* announced that "George Washington Carver, the latches of whose shoes few white men in Oklahoma are worthy to unlatch, must warm himself in the corner of a Jim Crow coach and suffer."

A flurry of editorials and letters condemned the railroad for racial segregation, but they also criticized Carver for not pushing the matter further. The head of the Atchison, Topeka and Santa Fe Railway had apologized and assured Carver that a similar incident would not happen again. Carver was satisfied with that response. Unfortunately, one month later another black man was denied a sleeping berth, and the ugly uproar resurfaced. Carver's fame could shine a spotlight on the discrimination, but it would take decades before policies changed.

To avoid such situations, Carver sometimes traveled by car. He did not know how to drive, so he relied on friends to chauffeur him around. They took picnic lunches with them so they didn't have to rely on finding a "colored only" restaurant. When the car broke down, Carver would wander off to collect a snack from the plants along the roadside. His drivers joked that when they ran out of gas, Carver could extract fuel from the nearby foliage.

Polio and Peanuts

Every summer there was an outbreak of poliomyelitis—polio—somewhere in the country. Polio is a devastating disease caused by a virus. It attacks the nervous system, weakening limbs in some patients and preventing others from breathing. Some people recover while others are paralyzed for life. Before Jonas Salk created a vaccine in 1955, doctors had no answers. They tried everything from braces to surgery and every kind of physical therapy to help their patients. Carver, who had always been a believer in massage therapy ever since he helped ease the soreness of football

Carver's favorite pastime was collecting plants. *Tuskegee University Archives, Tuskegee University*

players at Iowa, tried massaging two polio patients with peanut oil. It did not cure them, but they found some relief in the weekly massages.

Thrilled by his patients' improvement, Carver mentioned it to a reporter from the Associated Press. Carver had not found a cure, and he was clear on that, but that didn't matter to the many

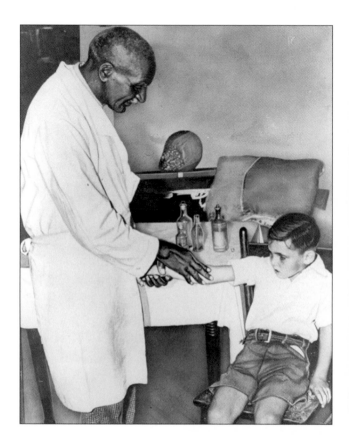

(above) **Carver examines a polio patient.** *Tuskegee University Archives, Tuskegee University*

(right) **Carver received hundreds of letters from polio patients.** *Tuskegee University Archives, Tuskegee University*

people who desperately needed good news. It was the middle of the Great Depression. A quarter of Americans were out of work. Many lost their homes and their farms. Folks grabbed at any good news they heard.

Soon sacks of letters arrived in Carver's office. By the end of the first month a mound of more than 1,000 letters dwarfed his desk. More people arrived in person to talk to the man the newspapers dubbed the peanut wizard. Carver grew exhausted answering each letter and meeting with each patient. He advised them to see a doctor, exercise, and rub their withered limbs with peanut

oil. It wasn't so much the peanut oil that improved muscle tone and feeling, but the rubbing action. His approach was similar to those of Sister Kenny, an Australian nurse who popularized massage therapy several years later.

Publicity surrounding Carver and his efforts helped shine a light on black polio patients. Doctors wrongly thought that African Americans were immune to the virus, but that was not the case. They suffered in silence because they were refused treatment at white hospitals. Franklin D. Roosevelt, who lost the use of his legs to polio, founded Warm Springs in Georgia in the 1920s, but they also barred black patients. In 1941, after a lot of protests and campaigning, the March of Dimes established a groundbreaking polio rehabilitation center at Tuskegee.

Carver Gets an Assistant

No one at Tuskegee had the packed schedule that Carver kept day in and day out. The college decided to give Carver, now in his seventies, an assistant. Many came and many went—quickly. Carver did not approve of any of them. He needed someone who understood his work and his methods. In the fall of 1935, Austin W. Curtis entered his office.

George Washington Carver meets President Roosevelt. *Tuskegee University Archives, Tuskegee University*

The Carver Meteorite

One day, a farmer from the county knocked on Carver's door. He had heard about Carver's rock collection and thought Carver might like to see what he had found in his field. Carver had seen a lot of rocks from farmers' fields, mostly small, gravelly bits of quartz and a lot of clay. But he politely followed the man outside. Carver must have been surprised to see a large, glossy black rock the size of one of his satchels. He probably

A slice of the Carver Meteorite. *Photo by author, courtesy of The Tuskegee University Archives, Tuskegee University*

knew right away what it was, especially when he and the farmer tried to pick it up, because it was considerably heavier than it looked—207 pounds. It was a meteorite, a chunk of a larger meteor, asteroid, or comet that survived the fall through the Earth's atmosphere. It became one of the biggest rocks in Carver's collection.

The meteorite was on display for many years at the Carver Museum at Tuskegee, until 1969, when the rock was moved to the Institute of Meteoritics at the University of New Mexico for study. Scientists classified the meteorite as one of the rarer types, made of iron and cobalt. Typically, meteorites are named after the place they were found, but Carver's rock was officially named the Carver Meteor. A slice of that meteor is now back at Tuskegee in the University archives, where it belongs.

Austin W. Curtis Jr.

Before Austin W. Curtis arrived at Tuskegee, he was a student at Cornell University. His degree in chemistry greatly enhanced Carver's research. Curtis worked with Carver for eight years and helped found the Carver Museum and the George Washington Carver Foundation. After Carver died, Curtis moved to Detroit, Michigan, and created Curtis Laboratories. He produced 60 hair and skin care products, many of which used peanut oil. He died in 1971.

Curtis was a recent graduate from Cornell University in New York. Carver told Curtis what he had told the other applicants: look around, introduce yourself to people. Although he didn't say it, he meant *don't bother me*.

Curtis was ideal. He wandered around and made himself useful grinding magnolia seeds and extracting the oil. He reported his progress to Carver who listened and nodded silently. George kept an eye on the young man's progress and liked what he saw. Wherever Carver went, Curtis was there to carry out an experiment, take notes, or simply lend a stable arm for the elderly professor to hang on to.

Fungus Research

One project they worked on was collecting fungus. Carver had been named an official collaborator for the USDA mycology (the study of fungi) and plant disease survey. Identifying all the organisms that destroy crops was and is an important function of the USDA, and even in his seventies Carver was still, as his mentor Pammel once said, "the best collector." Carver added 303 specimens to the national collection in 1935, and 335 in 1936. All together he added more than 1,000 specimens to the US National Fungus Collection, which is located in Beltsville, Maryland. Some of the fungi George found included those that thwart gardeners and farmers today: powdery mildew, rust fungus, and smut fungus, as well as all sorts of mushrooms. Several were even named after him, including *C. carveriana* and *P. carveri*.

One More Insult

In 1939, at the height of his fame, Carver still encountered discrimination. On a trip to New York City to speak on a radio show, Carver and Curtis arrived at the hotel where Curtis had made a reservation. The clerk at the desk said they did not have a room available. Carver might have left to find a more amiable hotel, but Curtis challenged the desk clerk. Hours went by. Carver grew more tired and sat in an alcove as Curtis called Doubleday, the book publisher who was publishing a biography on Carver. Doubleday talked to the hotel manager who still insisted that every room was occupied. But when an employee of Doubleday walked in and asked for a room he was promptly given one. Six hours they waited until they were given a room.

This kind of treatment was beginning to take its toll on Carver, but he still worried about his message more than himself. He wrote a friend, "Please pray for me that I may say the right thing in the right way at all times."

Carver on the radio.
Tuskegee University Archives, Tuskegee University

A Renewed Vision

Carver had known about Henry Ford, the founder of the Ford Motor Company, for many years. Ford created the Model T, established the five-dollar-a-day wage for his workers, and installed an assembly line that cranked out affordable cars for the average American.

But it wasn't until 1935 that Carver discovered how much he had in common with the white millionaire car manufacturer. Both men grew up on a farm, Carver in Missouri and Ford in Michigan. Both men believed that education for all citizens would lift up the nation. And both men hated waste. They were believers in reduce, reuse,

Carver had a keen eye for unusual plants and fungi. *Tuskegee University Archives, Tuskegee University*

Make a Spore Print

A mushroom is the fleshy fruiting part of a fungus that grows out of the ground. Inside the gills of a mushroom cap are thousands of tiny spores, or seeds. Spore color helps mycologists (scientists who study fungi) identify mushrooms. To determine the color, scientists make a spore print.

YOU'LL NEED

- Mushroom (one from the grocery store works well)
- Scissors
- White paper
- Bowl larger than the mushroom

1. Carefully take the stem out of the mushroom without damaging the gills underneath. If the mushroom has a lot of flesh covering the gills, use scissors to trim off the edge.

2. Find an out-of-the-way flat surface, and place the mushroom, gill side down, on the paper. Cover with an overturned bowl to prevent any breeze from disturbing the spores. Let it sit overnight.

3. Carefully remove the bowl and the mushroom to reveal your print.

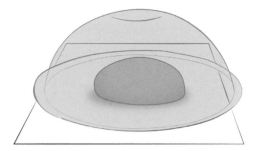

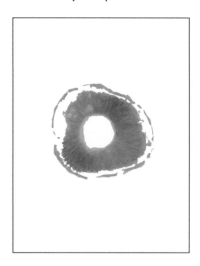

If your mushroom has light-colored gills, try placing it on dark-colored paper for a more distinct print.

recycle long before it became a catchy slogan. While Carver worked on a small scale, teaching a farmer's wife how to make rugs out of corn stalks, Ford worked on an industrial scale, turning a factory full of sawdust into charcoal briquettes. Both men had also been consulted by the US government about finding an American-grown substitute for rubber.

Ford knew about Carver too. Ford had been following the innovative research coming out of Tuskegee for years, but the two had never met. In 1935 Ford invited Carver to speak at the first chemurgy conference. *Chemurgy* (meaning chemistry at work) was a newly coined word given to the science of finding new ways to use agricultural crops in industry. This was something Carver had been practicing for years. Finally, the scientific world had caught up with him.

Unable to make it that year due to illness, the two elderly men, both in their seventies, wrote back and forth and developed a fond friendship. They met for the first time in 1937. Carver's failing health made travel more difficult. Staying up all night in a "colored only" train car was no longer an option. Ford was so eager to have Carver at the conference that he sent a private train car down to Tuskegee to pick him up and prepared a room for him at the Dearborn Inn where all the other guests were staying.

When the train arrived, Carver stepped onto the platform and Ford was there to greet him. Carver followed in the flurry of Ford's excitement. Ford showed him the soybean laboratory where for five years Ford's team had been working on

Carver meets Henry Ford. *Tuskegee University Archives, Tuskegee University*

new uses for soybeans. As they picked their way through beakers and Bunsen burners, Carver told Ford about his experiments with soybeans in 1904. Carver told Ford he preferred the peanut and sweet potato. Like the soybean, they were easy to grow, nourished the soil, and provided a source of protein to a farmer's diet. For lunch that day, Carver and Ford ate an all soy-based meal and enjoyed a

Carver and Curtis at work. *Tuskegee University Archives, Tuskegee University*

soybean ice cream cone for dessert. Their friendship overlooked a disparity in wealth and a difference in skin color. It was focused on intellect and ideas, which both men had in abundance.

Ford showed them the specially designed lab that he created just for Carver's visit. Carver and Curtis stayed in Michigan for a month working in the lab on projects he and Ford thought up.

When Carver returned to Tuskegee, he wrote Ford a letter. "I was thrilled and inspired as never before," he said. "I have been able to work better, you seem to be ever present with me in my investigations." Carver went on to investigate the medical uses of persimmons and Osage oranges. Synthetic rubber was again on his "to-do" list. And just in time.

World War II

By 1939 the world was at war again. Germany had invaded Poland and soon controlled much of Europe. The United States government launched another conservation effort, encouraging citizens to save paper, tin, gasoline, and bacon grease. The government issued food stamps for sugar, bread, and butter. Suddenly Carver's research became relevant again. Most of the synthetic rubber used during the war was made from grain alcohol from agricultural crops. The sweet potato provided the starch for laundering uniforms, and the US Postal Service used sweet potato–based glue on the back of postage stamps.

When coconut oil was too difficult to get from the Philippines, Carver was asked if peanut oil could replace it in soap. Paint manufacturers sought an oil substitute also. Carver devised an ingenious way to make paint by recycling discarded motor oil. He experimented with at least six different formulas before he found the best method.

Building a Museum

At 75 years old, Carver was busier than ever. Even so, he knew that his work was coming to an end. Yet he saw a bright future for those who would follow in his footsteps. In a speech he gave called "Chemistry and Peace," Carver said, "The ideal chemist of the future will be an investigator, one who dares to think and work with an independent freedom." They will create "new and useful products from material almost or quite beneath our feet and now considered of little or no value."

Carver may have been talking about the future, but he was also describing his past. For years he had toiled in his lab regardless of what others thought of his results. His products, although not utilized to the extent that they could have been, were the products of his firm belief in recycling and working in partnership with nature. This was the legacy he wanted to leave behind. The best way to do that, he thought, was to create a research foundation to fund future scientists, and a museum to house all his exhibits, products, and processes. He deeded his life savings, more than $33,000, to the project.

For a man who earned his living in his early years washing other people's clothes it was fitting

The George Washington Carver Museum. *Photo by author*

that his museum would be housed in the school's former laundry facility. Carver took his cue from Henry Ford's Greenfield Village. Ford bought historically significant buildings such as the Wright Brothers' bicycle shop, or reconstructed others like Thomas Edison's laboratory, and set them up in his makeshift village. Similarly, Carver recreated his laboratory and displayed paint samples, jars of preserved fruits and vegetables, dozens of peanut and sweet potato products, the skeleton of Betsy the ox, his rock collection, rugs made from cotton stalks, pots made out of clay, and samples of edible weeds. One biographer called it "an encyclopedia of Southern potentialities."

Pernicious anemia, a condition Carver had struggled with on and off his whole life, weakened his aging body. Shots of vitamin B12 got him on his feet for short bursts. When he felt good enough, Carver ambled from his apartment to work at the museum, but many days he was too weak to leave his bed. His friend Ford installed an elevator in Dorothy Hall where Carver lived so he would not have to tire himself on the stairs.

Carver continued to use the microscope his Iowa colleagues gave him. *Tuskegee University Archives, Tuskegee University*

Curtis answered the letters that continued to flood in from all over the world—no, he could not speak at your conference, and yes, he was feeling much better.

It was obvious to everyone that Carver was slowing down. A bit more hunched, he looked like a turtle huddled over his microscope. As Carver grew weaker he also grew more reclusive, annoyed by people who just wanted to gawk at the peanut man. Through it all he kept his sense of humor. When one reporter wrote that he was a toothless old man, Carver said it was nonsense. "I had my teeth right in my pocket the whole time."

In December 1942 Carver fell while trying to open the door to the museum. "The awful tragedy of my falling has thoroughly upset me," he said, "as I remain sore from head to foot yet." Two weeks later, in the evening of January 5, 1943, Carver died peacefully in his bed. He was almost 80 years old.

He Blazed a Trail

In many ways, George Washington Carver was ahead of his time. He believed in helping the poorest people in America when the nation was systematically keeping them down. He pushed for conservation, sustainable agriculture, and organic farming long before they were popular ideas. But this was all consistent with the way he viewed the world and his place in it. It was all connected. Carver was connected to the earth; therefore, he nurtured it and taught others to care for the land. He felt a connection to all mankind; therefore, he cared for others and sought to raise them up.

Carver felt these connections as a boy on the Carver farm in Missouri. He relied on them as he traveled alone across the Midwest. College labeled his childhood beliefs—ecology and conservation. Science gave him the means to explore these connections at the chemical level. Finally, the Tuskegee Institute gave Carver the platform to spread his message to the world.

"I am a blazer of trails. . . . Others must take up the various trails of truth and carry them on." —George Washington Carver

If Carver were alive today he'd be called an agricultural engineer, a materials engineer, or a biochemist like the many researchers who have followed in his footsteps creating new ways to use farm crops. Today we have biodegradable packaging made from bamboo and bulrush, and gasoline blended with ethanol produced from corn and sugar cane. Soybeans are turned into ink, crayons, lotions, and dozens of other products, and the hulls of Carver's lowliest peanuts are used in potting soil, livestock bedding, fireplace logs, wallboard, and paper.

Carver would be pleased.

George Washington Carver.
Tuskegee University Archives, Tuskegee University

A Lifetime of Honors and Awards

While Carver was alive he received several honors for his contributions to science and to improving race relations. After his death in 1943 he continued to be recognized as an important figure in American history.

1916	Fellow, London Royal Society for the Encouragement of the Arts
1923	NAACP Spingarn Medal for Distinguished Service to Science
1928	Honorary Degree, Doctor of Science, Simpson College
1939	Roosevelt Medal for Outstanding Contribution to Southern Agriculture
	Honorary Membership, American Inventors Society
1941	Honorary Degree, University of Rochester
1941	Award of Merit, Variety Clubs of America
1942	Honorary Degree, Doctor of Science, Selma University
1943	George Washington Carver National Monument (first non-president to receive)
1946	January 5 designated George Washington Carver Day
1947	US Postal Service issues George Washington Carver 3¢ stamp
1951–1954	US Mint issues George Washington Carver 50¢ coin
1952	Polaris submarine named USS *George Washington Carver*
1977	Enshrined, Hall of Fame for Great Americans
1990	Inducted into the National Inventors Hall of Fame
1998	US Postal Service issues Carver 32¢ stamp

Dozens of schools and scholarships named after George Washington Carver

ACKNOWLEDGMENTS

It has been a privilege and joy to meet so many wonderful people excited and eager to share their knowledge about George W. Carver. A special thank you to Curtis Gregory, park ranger at the George Washington Carver National Monument, for his insight into George's early years, for trusting me with a rare book, and for locating photographs and primary documents. At Tuskegee University, Dana R. Chandler, University archivist, helped me understand the world George inhabited. Thank you for the information, the food, and the friendship. I am also grateful to Edith Powell, a skilled researcher in the Tuskegee University Archives, for guiding me through boxes of documents and sharing wonderful stories of George and the institute. Digital archival intern Jared McWilliams showed me dozens of photographs. Thank you for your patience.

For additional photographs, thank you to: Olivia Garrison, reference coordinator, Special Collections and University Archives, Iowa State University Library in Ames, Iowa; Dana Adkins-Heljeson, Kansas Geological Survey in Lawrence, Kansas; Holly E. Baker, chief of Interpretation & Resource Management at the Fort Scott National Historic Site in Fort Scott, Kansas; Tim Noakes, head of Public Services, Department of Special Collections at Stanford University in Stanford, California; John C. Konzal, archivist at the State Historical Society of Missouri Columbia Research Center in Columbia, Missouri; Cynthia (Cyd) M. Dyer, college librarian/archivist/professor at Dunn Library Simpson College in Indianola, Iowa; Marty Vestecka Miller and Dell Darling at the Nebraska State Historical Society in Lincoln, Nebraska; Alex Fejfar, research and media specialist at Ames Historical Society in Ames, Iowa; Cassie Ball, Ness County Clerk's Office in Ness County, Kansas; Jason E. Tomberlin, head of Research & Instructional Services at Wilson Special Collections Library, University of North Carolina at Chapel Hill; Shirley Baxter, park ranger at the Tuskegee Institute National Historic Site, Tuskegee, Alabama; and never-ending gratitude to Francis Thomas for everything.

GEORGE WASHINGTON CARVER

RESOURCES TO EXPLORE

PLACES TO VISIT IN PERSON OR ONLINE

George Washington Carver National Monument

5646 Carver Road, Diamond, Missouri 64840

www.nps.gov/gwca/

Follow the trail over the creek where George caught frogs, visit the Carver house and gravesite, and stand in a replica of Carver's Tuskegee lab.

George Washington Carver National Museum and Tuskegee National Historic Site

1212 West Montgomery Road, Tuskegee Institute, Alabama 36088

www.nps.gov/tuin/

View George's paintings, a portion of his rock collection, Betsy the ox, Alabama clay paint samples, his microscope, lab equipment, and a replica of the Jesup Wagon.

Neosho Colored School Historic Site

639 Young Street, Neosho, Missouri 64650

This is the location of what was historically known as the Neosho Colored School that George attended in 1876. The Watkinses' house where George lived is no longer standing.

George Washington Carver Homestead Site

One mile south of Beeler, Kansas 67518

www.kansastravel.org/gwcarverbeeler.htm

A small plaque honoring Carver's achievements and his time in Beeler is located in the northeast corner of the land he once owned.

Ottawa County Historical Museum

110 South Concord Street, Minneapolis, Kansas 67467

www.kansastravel.org/ottawacountymuseum.htm

Tour the artifacts and exhibits about George's time in Minneapolis.

Bust of George W. Carver at the George Washington Carver National Monument in Diamond, Missouri. *Photo by author*

BOOKS

Burchard, Peter Duncan. *Carver: A Great Soul*. Fairfax, CA: Serpent Wise, 1998.

Collier, Christopher, and James Lincoln Collier. *Reconstruction and the Rise of Jim Crow 1864–1896*. New York: Cavendish Square, 2000.

Harkness, Cheryl. *The Ground-breaking, Chance-taking Life of George Washington Carver and Science and Invention in America*. Washington, DC: National Geographic For Kids, 2008.

Nelson, Marilyn. *Carver: A Life in Poems*. Honesdale, PA: Wordsong, 2001.

WEBSITES

Tuskegee University Archives for rare recordings of George speaking: http://archive.tuskegee.edu/archive/handle/123456789/936

Growing a Nation; the story of American Agriculture: https://agclassroom.org/gan/

The State Historical Society of Missouri; Famous Missourians: http://shsmo.org/historicmissourians/name/c/carver/

Library of Congress, America's Story; George Washington Carver: http://www.americaslibrary.gov/aa/carver/aa_carver_subj.html

National Peanut Board: http://nationalpeanutboard.org/peanut-info/george-washington-carver.htm

Iowa State University Library Digital Collections: http://digitalcollections.lib.iastate.edu/george-washington-carver/biography

National Park Service, American Visionaries, Legends of Tuskegee: https://www.nps.gov/museum/exhibits/tuskegee/

NOTES

CHAPTER 1: ALL THAT IS KNOWN

"No individual has any right": Carver, letter to Booker T. Washington, May 25, 1915, GWC Collection, TUA.

"As nearly as I can trace": Carver, "1897 or Thereabouts," 1, GWCNM Archives.

"freedom was declared": Carver, letter to Louis Pammel, May 5, 1922, GWC Collection, ISU Archives.

"This is all that is known": Carver, letter to C. H. Pearson, January 24, 1941, GWC Collection, TUA.

"negro girl named Mary": bill of sale, October 9, 1855, GWC Collection, TUA.

"sound in body and mind": bill of sale, October 9, 1855, GWC Collection, TUA.

"I am told that my father": Carver, "A Brief Sketch of My Life," 1, GWCNM Archives.

"I was so very frail": Carver, "A Brief Sketch of My Life," 1, GWCNM, Archives.

"as a little boy": Carver, quoted in *St. Louis Post Dispatch*, March 1942.

"scoured the wool": Carver, letter to Allen Eaton, January 16, 1940, GWC Collection, TUA.

"I never saw anybody": Carver, miscellaneous quotations, GWC Collection, TUA.

"dearest boyhood playmate": Carver, letter to Eva Goodwin, January 25, 1929, GWCNM Archives.

"Indeed you really are": Carver, letter to Eva Goodwin, January 25, 1929, GWCNM Archives.

"I almost knew": Carver, "A Brief Sketch of My Life," 1, GWCNM Archives.

"I literally lived": Carver, "A Brief Sketch of My Life," 1, GWCNM Archives.

"I obeyed": Carver, "1897 or Thereabouts," 1, GWCNM Archives.

No problem is too big: Carver, unpublished manuscript, GWC Collection, TUA.

"Rocks had an equal": Carver, "1897 or Thereabouts," 1, GWCNM Archives.

"I have some": Carver, "1897 or Thereabouts," 1, GWCNM Archives.

"Day after day": Carver, "1897 or Thereabouts," 1, GWCNM Archives.

"And many are the tears": Carver, "1897 or Thereabouts," 1, GWCNM Archives.

"Look about you": Hersey, *My Work*, 187.

"Strange to say": Carver, "1897 or Thereabouts," 1, GWCNM Archives.

"an exceptionally brilliant boy": Toogood, *Historic Resource Study*, 26.

CHAPTER 2: AMONG STRANGERS

"wafted hither and thither": Carver, letter to Miss Clopton, undated, GWC Collection, TUA.

"They encouraged me": Carver, "1897 or Thereabouts," 1, GWCNM Archives.

"perfectly willing for us": Carver, "A Brief Sketch of My Life," 2, GWCNM Archives.

"They don't realize": Carver, letter to Miss Clopton, GWC Collection, TUA.

"I like to hear myself": Vella, *George Washington Carver*, 22.

"each summer Mariah": Susan Richards Johnson & Associates, Inc., *Historic Structure Report*, 34.

"Indeed Mr. and Mrs. Watkins": Gart, *He Shall Direct Thy Paths*, 60.

"in a narrow buggy": Gart, *He Shall Direct Thy Path*, 61.

"Toot, toot honey": Susan Richards Johnson & Associates, Inc., *Historic Structure Report*, 38.

"Oh it was a big problem": Fuller, Amelia Richardson Interview, 2, GWCNM Archives.

"did not have much": Jefferson, "Recalls Carver's Life," 1, GWCNM Archives.

"He was held in high regard": Susan Richards Johnson & Associates, Inc., *Historic Structure Report*, 23.

"This simply sharpened": Carver, "1897 or Thereabouts," 2, GWCNM Archives.

"I was anxious to go": Gart, *He Shall Direct Thy Paths*, 63.

"he was very smart": Fuller, Amelia Richardson interview, 1, GWCNM Archives.

"Learn all you can": Gart, *He Shall Direct Thy Paths*, 61.

"When they heard from me": Carver, "1897 or Thereabouts," 2, GWCNM Archives.

"and amid thundering yells": Gart, *He Shall Direct Thy Paths*, 64.

"in a fire of dry goods boxes": Gart, *He Shall Direct Thy Paths*, 64.

"As young as I was": Gart, *He Shall Direct Thy Paths*, 65.

"He was quiet": Gart, *He Shall Direct Thy Paths*, 67.

"The sad news": Carver, "A Brief Sketch of My Life," 2, GWCNM Archives.

"You can be served": McMurry, *Scientist & Symbol*, 24.

"I was knocked silly": Carver, *Better Way*, GWCNM Archives.

"The thirst for knowledge": Carver, "1897 or Thereabouts," 2, GWCNM Archives.

"When the President saw": Carver, "A Brief Sketch of My Life," 2, GWCNM Archives.

"shall reside upon": homestead application, GWCNM Archives.

"I have seen him": Gart, *He Shall Direct Thy Paths*, 81.

"were able to look": Carver, letter to O. L. Lennen, GWCNM Archives.

"When I was in": McMurry, *Scientist & Symbol*, 27.

"He is a pleasant": *Ness County News*, March 31, 1888, GWCNM Archives.

CHAPTER 3: A REAL HUMAN BEING

"When you can do": Merritt, *From Captivity*, 58.

"I cooked at this hotel": Carver, "A Brief Sketch of My Life," 3, GWCNM Archives.

"The next day": Carver, "A Brief Sketch of My Life," 3, GWCNM Archives.

"I had to sing": Carver, "A Brief Sketch of My Life," 3, GWCNM Archives.

"Whoever heard of": Carver, "A Brief Sketch of My Life," 3, GWCNM Archives.

"sent one of the girls": Carver, letter to Mrs. Millholland, August 16, 1918, GWCNM Archives.

"It was my decision": Carver, letter to Mrs. Millholland, August 16, 1918, GWCNM Archives.

"feeling very much depressed" . . . *"'I will'"*: Carver, letter to Mrs. Milholland, August 16, 1918, GWCNM Archives.

"I lived on these": Carver, "A Brief Sketch of My Life," 3, GWCNM Archives.

"an [original] design": Carver, letter to Mrs. Milholland, undated, GWCNM Archives.

"I have wanted": Gart, *He Shall Direct Thy Paths*, 81.

"I am taking better care": Carver, letter to Mrs. Milholland, April 8, 1890, GWCNM Archives.

"we saw so much": McMurry, *Scientist & Symbol*, 28.

"They made me believe": McMurry, *Scientist & Symbol*, 28.

"liked Mr. Carver": Hersey, *My Work*, 28.

"I as yet do not": Carver, letter to Mrs. Milholland, August 6, 1891, GWCNM Archives.

"the next day everything": McMurry, *Scientist & Symbol*, 33.

"must understand his soil": Hersey, *My Work*, 31.

"It was he": Hersey, *My Work*, 30.

"a magic touch": McMurry, *Scientist & Symbol*, 35.

"Nature does not": Carver, "Grafting the Cacti," 1, GWC Collection, ISUA.

"Each created thing": Hersey, *My Work*, 42.

"was the most wonderful": Hersey, *My Work*, 44.

"As the Chemist" . . . *"assist her in her work"*: Carver, "Plants as Modified by Man," 1, GWC Collection, ISUA.

"difficult, in fact impossible": Holt, *An American Biography*, 95.

"by the productions": Washington, Atlanta Exposition Address, September 18, 1895.

"It has always been": Carver, letter to Booker T. Washington, April 12, 1896, GWC Collection, TUA.

"the best equipped": Washington, letter to Carver, April 17, 1896, GWC Collection, TUA.

"I will accept the offer": Carver, letter to Booker T. Washington, April 21, 1896, GWC Collection, TUA.

"cast down your bucket": Washington, Atlanta Exposition Address, September 18, 1895.

CHAPTER 4: TUSKEGEE

"Is the problem": Carver, unpublished manuscript, GWC Collection, TUA.

"When my train left": Kremer, *George Washington Carver*, 79.

"The scraggly cotton": Kremer, *George Washington Carver*, 79.

"Everything looked hungry": Kremer, *George Washington Carver*, 79.

"8:00 to 9:00 agri.": Carver, letter to Booker T. Washington, January 20, 1904, GWC Collection, TUA.

"I came knowing that": Carver, letter to Booker T. Washington, January 20, 1904, GWC Collection, TUA.

"Now Mr. Washington": Carver, letter to Booker T. Washington, May 30, 1898, GWC Collection, TUA.

"Who is that funny": Turner, interview, Documenting the American South, Southern Oral History Program.

"This old notion": Carver, letter to Booker T. Washington, December 19, 1898, GWC Collection, TUA.

"A large part of": Carver, *Nature Study Bulletin*, 3, GWC Collection, TUA.

"a humbug": McMurry, *Scientist & Symbol*, 99.

"requires the highest intelligence": Hersey, *My Work*, 105.

"time to say a kind": Parks, letter to Carver, July 16, 1917, GWC Collection, TUA.

"You'd always try" . . . *"but you don't see"*: Turner, interview, Documenting the American South, Southern Oral History Program.

"a great teacher": Washington, letter to Carver, February 26, 1911, GWC Collection, TUA.

"There is nothing better": Hersey, *My Work*, 103.

"There is nothing that": Carver, *Nature Study*, 22, GWC Collection, TUA.

"The Tuskegee station": Carver, *How to Build*, 4, GWC Collection, TUA.

"had but little to": Carver, *How to Build*, 4, GWC Collection, TUA.

"A poor soil produces": Hersey, *My Work*, 194.

"Many thousands of dollars": Hersey, *My Work*, 139.

"pine tops, hay": Carver, *How to Build*, 4, GWC Collection, TUA.

"Nature has provided": Burchard, *Carver: A Great Soul*, 149.

"A good plate": Hersey, *My Work*, 133.

"A soil's deficiency": Carver, *Cow Peas*, 3, GWC Collection, TUA.

"As a food for": Carver, "Possibilities," 1910, GWC Collection, TUA.

"The primary idea": Merritt, *From Captivity to Fame*, 24.

"It is just as important": Hersey, *My Work*, 131.

"Coffee from Brazil": Kremer, *George Washington Carver*, 118.

"The Man to Answer": advertisement for Farmers' Picnic, GWC Collection, TUA.

"If your soil": advertisement for Farmers' Picnic, GWC Collection, TUA.

"put a few tools": Hersey, *My Work*, 149.

"No. I came to": Campbell, *The Movable School*, 47.

"Sure. That sounds": Campbell, *The Movable School*, 48.

"aid the farmer": Carver, *White and Color Washing*, 5, GWC Collection, TUA.

"as to whether": Carver, letter to Booker T. Washington, November 28, 1902, GWC Collection, TUA.

"to flee for his life": Carver, letter to Booker T. Washington, November 28, 1902, GWC Collection, TUA.

"the most frightful": Carver, letter to Booker T. Washington, November 28, 1902, GWC Collection, TUA.

CHAPTER 5: PEANUT FAME

"How far you go": George Washington National Monument.

"I am sure Mr. Washington": Carver, letter to Emmett Scott, February 15, 1916, GWC Collection, TUA.

"that was the best lecture": Hersey, *My Work*, 119.

"which is possessed": Hersey, *My Work*, 119.

"The most striking": McMurry, *Scientist & Symbol*, 150.

"So you see": Carver, letter to Mr. Hardwick, January 30, 1927, GWC Collection, TUA.

"field hand than": McMurry, *Scientist & Symbol*, 155.

"I don't want to": McMurry, *Scientist & Symbol*, 157.

"Not one time": Carver, letter to A. L. Holsey, January 24, 1918, GWC Collection, TUA.

"Food will win the war": WWI ad campaign.

"We must do": McMurry, *Scientist & Symbol*, 170.

"My work is that": Carver, "A Few Notes," 1, GWC Collection, TUA.

"It is estimated": Carver, *When, What*, 3, GWC Collection, TUA.

"We are richer": Hersey, *My Work*, 143.

"I think I am": Carver, letter to Walter M. Grubbs, October 1, 1919, GWC Collection, TUA.

"Dr. Carver verily": McMurry, *Scientist & Symbol*, 172.

"In profound appreciation": Plaque on the Boll Weevil Monument.

"This man": Kremer, *George Washington Carver*, 103.

"Your time is unlimited": Kremer, *George Washington Carver*, 107.

"I am very sorry" . . . *"protect a good thing"*: Kremer, *George Washington Carver*, 107.

"clear thought and straightforward": McMurry, *Scientist & Symbol*, 199.

"I am away from": McMurry, *Scientist & Symbol*, 205.

"Without genuine love": McMurry, *Scientist & Symbol*, 210.

"There is no better": McMurry, *Scientist & Symbol*, 205.

"no question": Hersey, *My Work*, 166.

"You have shown": McMurry, *Scientist & Symbol*, 214.

"No books ever go": Hersey, *My Work*, 180.

"Men of Science": Hersey, *My Work*, 180.

"Inspiration is never": Hersey, *My Work*, 180.

"dozens of things": Kremer, *George Washington Carver*, 130.

"If this is not": Kremer, *George Washington Carver*, 130.

"Science is simply the truth": Kremer, *George Washington Carver*, 130.

"George Washington Carver": McMurry, *Scientist & Symbol*, 227.

"the best collector": Pammel, letter to L. D. McCullough, November 3, 1928, LMP Collection, ISUA.

"Please pray for me": Carver, letter to J. Hardwick, GWC Collection, ISUA.

"I was thrilled": Skrabec, *The Green Vision*, 8.

"The ideal chemist": Carver, "Chemistry and Peace," 1, GWC Collection, TUA.

"an encyclopedia of": Holt, *An American Biography*, 327.

"I had my teeth": Holt, *An American Biography*, 328.

"The awful tragedy": McMurry, *Scientist & Symbol*, 302.

"I am a blazer": McMurry, *Scientist & Symbol*, 290.

SELECTED BIBLIOGRAPHY

ARCHIVES

George Washington Carver National Monument Archives

Iowa State University Archives, George Washington Carver Collection

Tuskegee University Archives, George Washington Carver Collection

BOOKS

Burchard, Peter Duncan. *Carver: A Great Soul*. Fairfax, CA: Serpent Wise, 1998.

Campbell, Thomas. *The Movable School Goes to the Negro Farmer*. Tuskegee, AL: Tuskegee Institute Press, 1936.

Gart, Jason H. *He Shall Direct Thy Paths: The Early Life of George W. Carver*. Diamond, MO: Historic Resource Study, George Washington Carver National Monument, 2014.

Hersey, Mark D. *My Work Is That of Conservation: An Environmental Biography of George Washington Carver*. Athens, GA: University of Georgia Press, 2011.

Holt, Rackham. *George Washington Carver: An American Biography*. New York: Doubleday, Doran, 1943.

Johnson, Susan Richards, & Associates. *Historic Structure Report, 1872 Neosho Colored School*. Kansas City, MO: Susan Richards Johnson & Associates, Inc., July 17, 2012. www.nps.gov/gwca/learn/management/upload/FINAL-REPORT-Neosho-Colored-School-HSR-8-31-12.pdf.

Kremer, Gary R. *George Washington Carver in His Own Words*. Columbia, MO: University of Missouri Press, 1987.

Mayberry, B. D. *A Century of Agriculture in the 1890 Land-Grant Institutions and Tuskegee University—1890–1990*. New York: Vantage Press, 1991.

Mayberry, B. D. *The Role of Tuskegee University in the Origin, Growth and Development of the Negro Cooperative Extension System 1881–1990*. Tuskegee, AL: Tuskegee University, 1989.

McMurry, Linda O. *George Washington Carver: Scientist & Symbol.* Oxford: Oxford University Press, 1981.

Merritt, Raleigh Howard. *From Captivity to Fame; or, The Life of George Washington Carver.* Boston: Meador Publishing Company, 1938.

Skrabec, Quentin R. Jr. *The Green Vision of Henry Ford and George Washington Carver: Two Collaborators in the Cause of Clean Industry.* Jefferson, NC: McFarland & Company, Inc., 2013.

INDEX

ISBN 978-1-55652-811-8
$17.99 (CAN $23.99)

America's Black Founders
Revolutionary Heroes & Early Leaders with 21 Activities

By Nancy I. Sanders

It's time to add the names Allen, Forten, and Hawley to the list that includes Washington, Jefferson, and Adams. From Crispus Attucks, the Revolutionary War's first martyr, to James Armistead Lafayette, a slave and spy who hastened the Continental Army's final victory over the British at the Battle of Yorktown, *America's Black Founders* honors the lesser-known but significant lives and contributions of our nation's early African American leaders.

Author Nancy I. Sanders tells the history of dozens of men and women—soldiers, sailors, ministers, poets, merchants, doctors, and other community leaders—who have earned proper recognition as founders of the United States of America. To get a better sense of what these individuals accomplished and the times in which they lived, readers will:

- Celebrate Constitution Day
- Cook a meal of pepper pot soup and firecakes
- Publish a newspaper
- Petition their government
- Craft a clay pot
- And much more

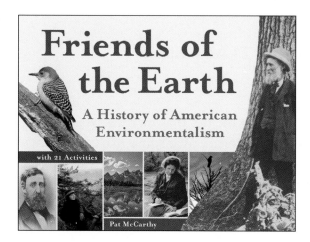

ISBN 978-1-56976-718-4
$16.95 (CAN $18.95)

Friends of the Earth
A History of American Environmentalism with 21 Activities

By Pat McCarthy

"Budding environmentalists will appreciate these accessible and inspiring biographies."
—*School Library Journal*

The history of American environmentalism is an inspiring story of men and women who dedicated their lives to protecting the nation's natural heritage. Cordelia Stanwood, and later Roger Peterson, revolutionized and popularized birdwatching. Almost singlehandedly, John James Audubon introduced the study of birds in North America, while John Muir pushed a president and a nation into setting aside vast preserves, including Yosemite, Sequoia, Mt. Rainier, and the Grand Canyon. Marjory Stoneman Douglas did the same for the Florida Everglades, as did Mardy Murie with the Grand Tetons and the Arctic National Wildlife Refuge. And Rachel Carson opened the world's eyes to the dangers of pesticides.

In addition to its engaging history, *Friends of the Earth* includes a time line of environmental milestones, a list of popular outdoor parks and sites to visit or explore online, and web resources for further study. Readers will also learn how to put their concerns into action. Kids will:

- Build two different types of birdfeeders
- Start a compost pile
- Study the greenhouse effect
- Make plaster casts of animals' tracks
- Plant a tree
- Test for acid rain
- And much more

ISBN 978-1-61373-146-8

$16.95 (CAN $19.95)

Henry David Thoreau for Kids
His Life and Ideas with 21 Activities

By Corinne Hosfeld Smith

"Well organized and with plenty of grist for both minds and hands." —*Kirkus Reviews*

Henry David Thoreau is best known for living two years along the shores of Walden Pond in Concord, Massachusetts, and writing about his experiences in *Walden; or, Life in the Woods.* Today, more than 150 years later, people are still inspired by his thoughtful words and observations about individual rights, social justice, civil disobedience, and the natural world.

Henry David Thoreau for Kids chronicles the short but influential life of this remarkable American thinker. In addition to learning about Thoreau's contributions to our culture, readers will participate in 21 engaging, hands-on projects that bring his ideas to life. Kids will:

- Build a model of the Walden cabin
- Keep a daily journal
- Plant a garden
- Bake trail-bread cakes
- Start a rock collection
- And much more!

The book also includes a time line and list of resources—books, websites, and places to visit or explore online—that offer even more opportunities to connect with this fascinating author and naturalist.

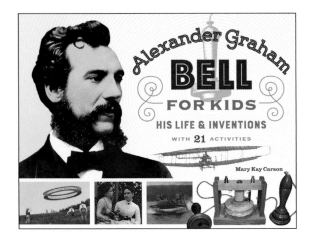

ISBN 978-0-912777-13-9
$16.99 (CAN $22.99)

Alexander Graham Bell for Kids
His Life & Inventions with 21 Activities

By Mary Kay Carson

"Children who enjoy exploring different symbolic communication codes, historical sciences, and inventions will find much to dig into in this detailed volume. Thorough and well-rounded."
—*Kirkus Reviews*

Alexander Graham Bell invented not only the telephone but also early versions of the phonograph, the metal detector, airplanes, and hydrofoil boats. This Scottish immigrant was also a pioneering speech teacher and a champion of educating those with hearing impairments, work he felt was his most important contribution to society. Bell worked with famous Americans such as Helen Keller and aviators Glenn Curtiss and Samuel P. Langley, and his inventions competed directly with those of Thomas Edison and the Wright Brothers.

This unique biography includes a time line, a list of online resources, and 21 engaging hands-on activities to better appreciate Bell's remarkable accomplishments. Kids will:

- Construct a Pie Tin Telegraph and a Pizza Box Phonograph
- "See" and "feel" sound by building simple devices
- Communicate using American Sign Language
- Send secret messages using Morse code
- Investigate the properties of ailerons on a paper airplane
- Build and fly a tetrahedral kite
- And more!

ISBN 978-1-61373-320-2
$16.99 (CAN $22.99)

Marie Curie for Kids
Her Life and Scientific Discoveries with 21 Activities and Experiments
By Amy M. O'Quinn

"An accessibly written, engaging introduction to a remarkable giant of science."
—*Kirkus Reviews*

Marie Curie, nicknamed "Manya" by her family, reveled in reading, learning, and exploring nature as a girl growing up in her native Poland. She went on to become one of the world's most famous scientists. Curie's revolutionary discoveries over several decades created the field of atomic physics, and Curie herself coined the word *radioactivity*. She was the first woman to win a Nobel Prize and the first person ever to win in two different fields—chemistry and physics.

Marie Curie for Kids introduces this legendary figure in all her complexity. Kids learn how Curie worked alongside her husband and scientific partner, Pierre, while also teaching and raising two daughters; how this intense scientist sometimes became so involved with her research that she forgot to eat or sleep; and how she struggled with health issues, refused to patent her discoveries (which would have made her very wealthy), and made valuable contributions during World War I.

Packed with historic photos, informative sidebars, a resource section, and 21 hands-on activities and experiments that illuminate Curie's life and work, *Marie Curie for Kids* is an indispensable resource for budding scientific explorers. Kids can:

- Examine real World War I X-rays
- Explore magnetism by making a simple compass
- Make a model of the element carbon
- Use the sun's rays to make art
- Make traditional Polish pierogies
- And much more

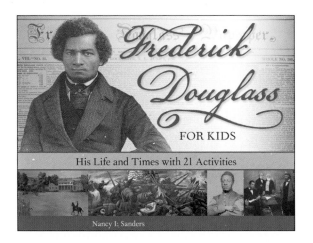

ISBN 978-1-56976-717-7
$16.95 (CAN $18.95)

Frederick Douglass for Kids
His Life and Times with 21 Activities

By Nancy I. Sanders

"Thoughtful and well-researched . . . a thorough and involving examination of a great man, equally suited to individual immersion and classroom collaboration." —*Booklist*

Few Americans have had as much impact on this nation as Frederick Douglass. Born on a plantation, he later escaped slavery and helped others to freedom via the Underground Railroad. In time he became a bestselling author, an outspoken newspaper editor, a brilliant orator, a tireless abolitionist, and a brave civil rights leader. He was famous on both sides of the Atlantic in the years leading up to the Civil War, and when war broke out, Abraham Lincoln invited him to the White House for counsel and advice.

Frederick Douglass for Kids follows the footsteps of a true hero, one of the leading African Americans of his day. And to better appreciate Douglass and his times, readers will:

- Form a debating club
- Create a sailor's tarpaulin hat and cravat that Douglass wore during his escape
- Make a Civil War haversack
- Participate in a microlending program
- And more

CHICAGO REVIEW PRESS

Available at your favorite bookstore, by calling (800) 888-4741, or at www.chicagoreviewpress.com